THE CATALYST

REIGNITE YOUR INNER FIRE

AMAN ARORA

I humbly dedicate this book to

My Mom & Dad

My brother Aryaman & sister Gorika

All those who have supported me in my good and bad
times.

And to all those suffering in silence,

Remember,

*"Until you spread your wings, you'll never know
how far you can FLY"*

Contents

PREFACE

I've had a rough patch in my life. Fear, Anxiety, stress have been a part of my life as far as i can remember. Various diseases caused due to my poor eating habits have lost me my valuable time.

While everything was going bad in my life and i was losing all my hope, I decided to lift myself up. I started to research on various psychological theories and came across a various range of articles written by some very learned people.

The lessons learned from these sources have transformed my life for better. They have provided me with self-confidence, helped me overcome my fear and anxiety.

Through this book, i plan on sharing some of the valuable lessons learnt by me in the past year.

I hope this book changes your life as it did mine

I
FACE YOUR MONSTERS

"Life Begins where Fear Ends"

Everyone experiences fear. It is an inevitable aspect of being human. While most of us regard it to be an unpleasant sensation, some of us go out of our way to provoke it. Sometimes there are legitimate reasons to feel afraid.

Fear has a long evolutionary history. We must credit fear for our existence as a species. Any animal that does not flee and hide from larger predators or risky circumstances would cease to exist.

Fear can make some of us behave recklessly but it is to aid us in our survival. In other words, if we are an facing a difficult situation, it makes sense to be a little cautious than to take everything for granted.

But this fear can also be irrational at times. Take an example of a horror movie. Even though we are aware that the ghost in a horror film is fake, we may still feel a surge of fear while viewing it.

৯৩

I often take inspiration from Bhagavad Gita to manage my emotions. It talks about how its main character, Prince Arjun, is coached by his charioteer, Lord Krishna, on the battlefield just before the first battle of the story. Arjun is advised by Krishna to put all fear aside and submit to him. Krishna says,

"पूरवृत्ततचि नविृततचि कार्याकार्य॑ भयाभय॑।
बंधं मोक्ष॑ च या वेत्ति बुद्धः सा पार्थ सात्त्वकिी ॥"

"*O Parth! The understanding by which one knows what is to be done and what is not to be done, what is to be feared and what is not to be feared, what is bondage and what is liberation is in the mode of goodness.*"

The conflict described in the Gita is uncannily comparable to many of our existing sentiments. Arjun's self-doubt, his troubled thoughts, and his paralyzing anxiety are exactly how our fears make us feel right now.

Krishna urges us to let go of our fears and reminds us that life is, in reality, a lovely experience meant to be experienced rather than feared. He instructs us to let go of our fears. He explains that it is fear which makes us human.

Fear, however, is not dispelled by the Bhagavad Gita. Instead, it diminishes it to a minor experience that is insignificant. Lord Krishna tells Arjun to set aside his worries and take action to carry out his responsibility as a warrior.

Krishna's message holds the truth in our life too. We all have some responsibilities to fulfill, a life to live, and memories to cherish. Thus, we shouldn't let our unnecessary emotions come into our way of life.

⁊৩

But if we are to overcome fear, we need to understand why we get scared. What happens in our body when we are frightened?

I think of it as a chemical reaction taking place in my brain. It gets triggered when I add a catalyst to a cocktail of emotions. Just like chemistry, this reaction is reversible and can be stopped by removing the catalyst.

The fight-or-flight response is a term used to describe the changes that take place in our body when we sense terror.

It begins when our adrenal gland releases epinephrine, commonly known as adrenalin and cortisol into our bloodstream. It causes an increase in white blood cells, blood sugar, and blood pressure. Fatty acids are converted into energy by the circulating cortisol, which is available for usage by the muscles in case of emergency. Muscles are made ready for violent action.

The pace of breathing and heartbeat picks up, the peripheral blood vessels, such those in the skin, constrict, while the central blood vessels around the critical organs widen to flood them with oxygen and nutrients.

A condition known as piloerection, or "goosebumps," is brought on by the tightening of muscles, including those at the root of each hair. Glucose levels in the blood grow as a result of metabolism, offering a fast source of energy should an emergency call for it.

Our pupils are dilated, tear and saliva production is suppressed causing us to have a dry mouth. It also produce tunnel vision, reduces our hearing, enhances our heart and lungs activity while decreasing activity in the stomach and intestines, generating the sensation of "butterflies" in the stomach. This is what we call 'FEAR'

All this happens the instant we sense fear. But what if our fear is unreasonable.

The prefrontal cortex and the hippocampus both assist in managing our fear response. They aid in our understanding of whether our fear response is reasonable or whether we may have slightly overreacted. They have the ability to reduce the severity of our fear response if they determine the reaction is excessive.

Some of us love viewing scary movies since our brain can suppress the natural fear reaction. We get to feel the rush of panic before our brain's more logical regions calm it down. We term it as 'Adrenaline Rush'

We can thus manage our fear by tricking our brain into thinking that the fear is unreasonable.

❧

We humans tend to have a dual nature by birth. Our emotions, including fear, are part of our lower nature. Our sub-conscious is the higher one. Even while facing intense fear, our consciousness remains fearless. We should always remember that we have a part of us that is never afraid. We have a switch inside of us that we can turn on and off to manage our emotions. When we start believing this, everything else is unnecessary.

Our head is made up of channels, both positive and negative. Whenever we feel fear, it opens up a negative channel. We can suppress it by opening up a new channel and drawing positive energies and ideas from it.

Whenever we feel afraid, we should remember what Krishna said:

> *"Him the weapons cannot cut, fire cannot burn, water cannot wet, wind cannot dry. The self cannot be cut, dried, burned or wetted... Eternal, all pervasive, stable, immovable, everlasting the Self Reigns"*

We have a brave part of ourself, we should never forget that. We should believe that courage is always available to assist us. It is comparable to a buddy who will give us their arm to lean on when things are tough.

When we keep in mind what Krishna said about the self being a friend to the self. Our consciousness will emerge to be our buddy and assist us in conquering our worries. We should conquer our fear by having faith and allowing it to be our most trustworthy ally.

> *"Kill the snake of doubt in our soul, crush the worms of fear in our heart and mountains will move out of our way."*

ॐ

Being fearless might look like a big challenge at first but when we start practising, it becomes a piece of cake. These tricks may help us in managing our fear.

ACT

We should try to take action instead of sitting back and doing nothing.

QUESTION

We should keep in mind that emotions are not facts. We should try to take charge of our life. Nothing can prevent us from taking action just because we are afraid of it. Identifying the root of our fear and discovering solutions might be the best thing to do.

THINK POSITIVE

Whenever we are facing fear, we should try to alter our perception in order to stop being afraid of it. We should thus take steps in the direction of the outcome we want to achieve by visualising it and acting on it.

LISTEN TO OUR THOUGHTS

We should try listening to our fearful thoughts rather than just accepting them as they are. Further, we should try to change the internal dialogue to a more uplifting one. We should give ourself the choice to either believe the thought or search for a more constructive and realistic alternative. We shouldn't try to tell ourself anything that will make us feel fearful, anxious, or stressed.

STOP

Whenever we have concerns that are harmful and irrational, such worrying constantly about something happening to our loved ones. The simplest method to deal with these worries when they arise is to just say, "Stop!" Once we have shown ourself that there is nothing we can do or that the most probable conclusion won't be the terrible event we anticipated.

DISTRACT

Another easy method for overcoming common phobias is distraction. We should use thought-stopping to halt the ideas, and then divert our attention to something more beneficial and constructive.

BREATHE

We should spend a few minutes in a quiet place doing some simple breathing exercises to help adjust as we try to conquer our fear. No matter what is going on around us, learning to breathe from our belly is a powerful method to quiet and centre ourself. Closing our eyes and taking few calm, deep belly breaths whenever we feel afraid can help us instantly.

BE AWARE OF OUR SURROUNDING

Paying attention to our surroundings by taking in the sights, sounds, feels, tastes, and scents using all of our senses. The more we employ this strategy, the simpler it will get to utilise it to reassure ourself that everything is okay at the moment when we are feeling afraid.

FIND THE ROOT OF THE STRESS

Finding the reason why we're having these feelings in the first place is one of the easiest strategies to overcome our worries.

EMBRACE

We should try to embrace our anxieties and accept them for what they are. They are a part of us no matter what, and addressing them rather than simply disregarding them is a terrific approach to get over them.

THE TAKEAWAY

"कृषतो नास्ति दुर्भिक्षं जपतो नास्ति पातकम्।
मौनतः कलहो नास्ति नास्ति जागरतो भयम्॥"

"With farming there is no famine. For one engaged in japa there is no sin. With silence there is no quarrel. For the wide awake there is no fear of theft"

The fear response has kept us alive. It is primal, and we should respect it. At the same time, it can be uncomfortable and obstruct us from going about our daily lives. There are no obstacles. If we think we can, there is nothing we cannot do. Yes, trying new things might be frightening, but if we don't take the chance, how can we discover the beauty that lies beyond the high walls of our life? We should go beyond our comfort zone with bravery because if we pass up the chance, we will regret it.

It is summarised beautifully by Vincent van Gogh,

"What would life be if we had no courage to attempt anything?"

II

THE STRESS THEORY

"Stress should be a powerful driving force, not an obstacle"

A short joyful moment may lift our spirits no matter what we may be going through?

There may be one or two friends in our life that can always make us laugh, even through the most difficult times. We often experience a reduction in stress at work after taking a break to chat with our favourite coworkers.

Putting our mind through the never-ending cycle of stress day in and day out has no positive effects. It may be draining and detrimental to our health. Chronic, continuing stress can harm our immune system as well as our creativity, drive, and productivity.

A chronically active stress response poses a major risk to our health. But if it's severe enough, even short-term stress can have a significant negative effect on our heart. Stress-induced cardiomyopathy or broken-heart syndrome is typically brought on by extreme mental or physical stress.

The stress chemicals cortisol, adrenaline, and epinephrine influence most regions of the body, producing sadness and anxiety, disrupting sleep, and raising the risk of stroke, high blood pressure, and heart disease. While certain forms of stress can be advantageous since they improve our ability to problem-solve and think rapidly, the majority of forms of stress are frequently unneeded and even hazardous to our health.

We regain the ability to be imaginative, focused, and resourceful when we are able to successfully eliminate stress in our life.

Let us try to understand stress with the help of "Yerkes-Dodson Law". It states that performance increases with increasing physiological or mental excitement for simple activities. However, if the work at hand is challenging, increasing arousal will only boost our performance up to a certain extent. After that, increased arousal will diminish our performance since we will be too nervous and anxious to focus on the job. Thus, we would normally do better at moderate levels of excitement.

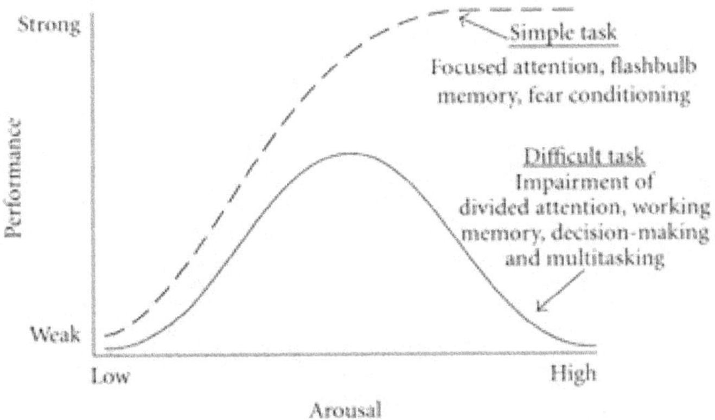

Yerkes-Dodson Curve

Video games typically conform exactly to the Yerkes-Dodson Law by placing us in situations or making us battle enemies who are neither too simple nor too difficult. That also explains why they could be addictive because being at our peak arousal feels good.

Paying attention to our body can help us start putting this theory into practise by letting us know what our ideal level of arousal is. We experience physical, mental, and emotional balance and comfort when we are at the ideal degree of arousal. We can choose what to do next more wisely if we are aware of our ideal degree of arousal.

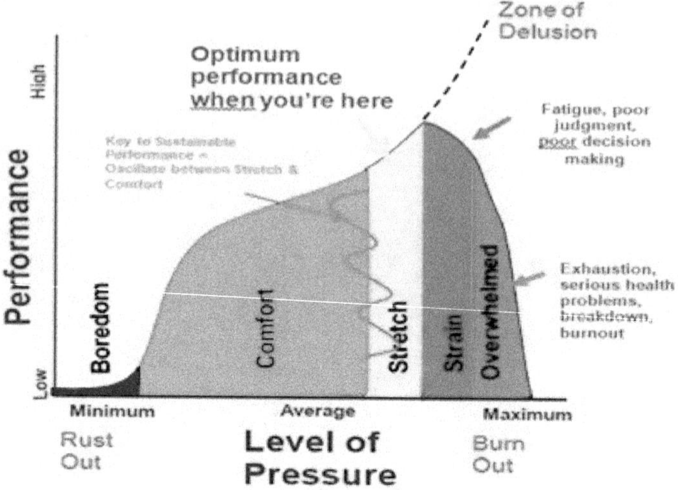

Performance Curve

Suppose, we have a challenging task and we are feeling excessively worried, we can consider altering our surroundings or our perspective so that it won't lead to further stress.

III

ANGER: A DISGUISE

"A heart filled with anger has no room for love"

Understanding the source of our anger and what lies beneath is critical for our own well-being and the well-being of others around us.

How can we be held accountable for our acts if we can't control them?

What is the most frequent primary emotion, or the initial feeling we feel before we experience anger?

What are we defending, and why?

Anger is a secondary emotion. We always feel another emotion first before we experience anger. The primary emotion is typically fear, sadness, or pain.

To overcome our anger, we need to explore what is being protected by our anger.

What is underneath that anger that is building a fortress so it does not have to be experienced?

What additional emotions are being felt?

What if we stayed with the initial feeling before switching to the protective mode of anger?

This type of activity may be quite beneficial in determining what truly causes our anger.

We discover that people are almost never the source of our rage.

Anger is nearly always fueled by a need to feel protected.

If we work on feeling safe, why would we need anger?

Have you ever wondered why we become enraged?

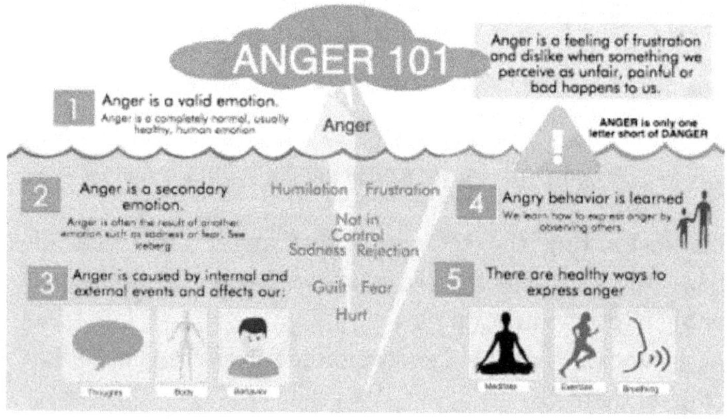

ANGER 101

"*Emotions are essentially action impulses, the quick strategies for dealing with life that evolution has placed in us.*"

Anger increases the flow of blood into our hands, making it simpler to hit an adversary or grip a weapon. Our heart rate increases and a burst of hormones creates a surge of energy powerful enough to justify aggressive action. Anger has been implanted in our brains in this way to protect us.

THE PURPOSE OF ANGER

Consider anger to be an iceberg. The majority of the iceberg is concealed beneath the water's surface. Similarly, when we are furious, we frequently have other emotions bubbling beneath the surface. It is simple to perceive anger, but it might be harder to recognize the underlying sentiments that the anger is shielding.

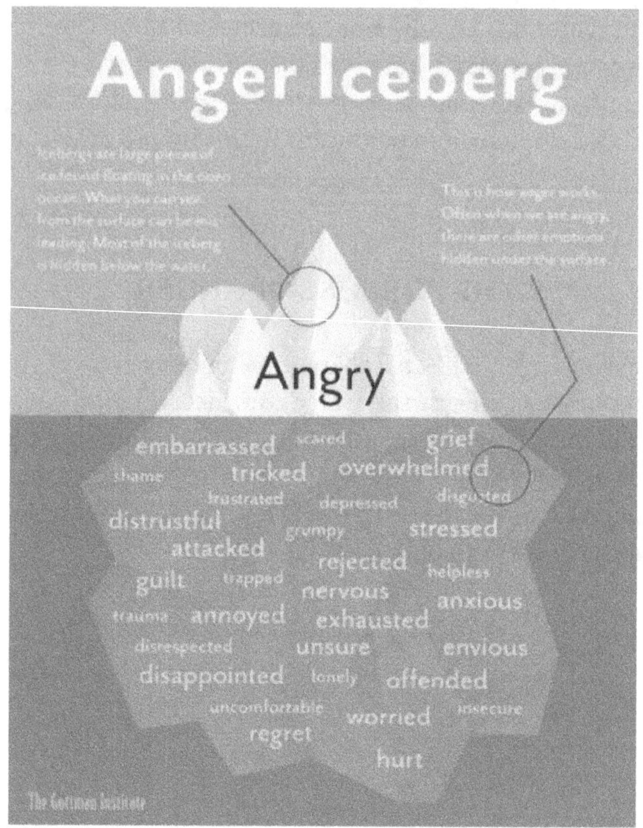

Anger Iceberg

Our intense emotions can serve as the messengers we require to teach us about ourselves and to trigger insights into critical life directions. There is something deeper behind the surface of our rage.

Anger is sometimes referred to be a "secondary emotion" because we use it to shelter ourselves from our own raw, vulnerable, and overpowering sensations. Anger is also one of the six "fundamental emotions" (anger, disgust, fear, happiness, sorrow, and surprise).

Everyone experiences anger at some time in their lives, and it is a fully legitimate emotion in its own right. But anger does not appear out of anywhere; it is frequently accompanied by other emotions or sentiments, which may lay beneath it.

Recognizing anger as a basic, genuine emotion as well as a guardian of our raw emotions may be quite effective. It can lead to restorative talks that can aid us in better understanding each other.

ॐ

TIPS FOR LISTENING TO ANGER

One of the most challenging aspects of listening to someone's anger, particularly when it is aimed at us, is that we feel defensive. As our own anger rises to the surface, we want to fight back. If this happens, we have a heated verbal argument that leaves both of us feeling misunderstood and upset.

The easiest approach to avoid this is to use some of the following suggestions.

Don't make it about Yourself

Someone else's anger has nothing to do with us. It's about their fundamental emotions. It requires a great level of emotional intelligence to not take this personally.

One method to accomplish this is to try to figure out why they're furious. It's a lot easy to get defensive, but when we attempt to think,

"Wow, this guy is upset, why is that?" we find it difficult. It will take us on a trip to witness the raw feelings they are shielding from us, bringing us closer to them.

NEVER, EVER tell someone to calm down

We should not try to modify or fix other people's feelings, but rather sit with them on their angry iceberg.

Make it clear that we understand and respect their sentiments. When we accomplish this correctly, their anger will fade and the core emotion will emerge. Not to mention that they will feel listened to, which will lead to increased trust over time.

Identify the obstacle

Anger is often caused by an obstacle blocking a goal.

ஐ

The simple line is that individuals are angry for a reason. It signals other emotions, but it is also a feeling in and of itself. It must be recognized. It is our responsibility to understand and sit with the other person in it. We will not only help them comprehend their anger, but we will also get closer to them as a result.

Showing anger allows us to protect our vulnerable feelings.

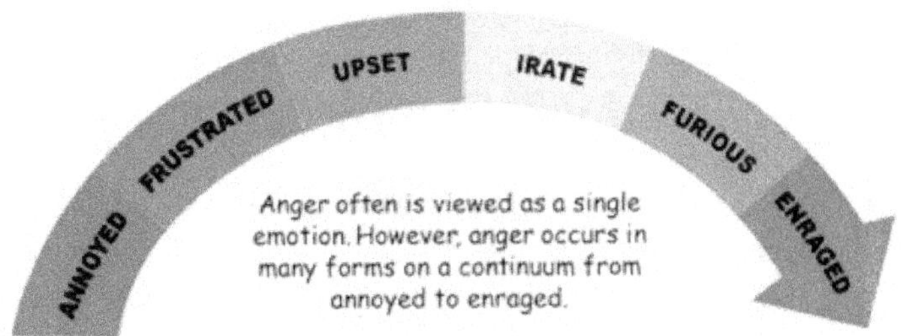

Stages of Anger

It may appear like a personal assault if someone says anything insulting, domineering, or humiliating to us. Because we are being treated in such a humiliating manner, we may experience fear, embarrassment, or sadness.

To feel more in control, we strike out in rage instead of addressing these sensitive thoughts that we perceive are weak. Unfortunately, violent behaviors such as screaming, throwing objects, shoving, or punching does not address our true feelings.

The next time we begin to feel angry, let us take a pause and think:

"What am I feeling underneath?"

Let us investigate the sadness, humiliation, jealousy, or fear that our anger is masking.

Let us consider the desired outcome of the scenario and the best strategy to achieve it. Our anger will fade as we take time to focus on our own ideas. We may need to count to ten or leave the room from time to time, but this is not a sign of weakness.

ॐ

ROOT OF ANGER

1. *SADNESS* can lead to anger if we don't allow ourselves to acknowledge and express the sorrow.

2. *FEAR*

3. *WORRY, and ANXIETY*

4. *FRUSTRATION* occurs when we think we are trapped and disempowered.

5. *DISAPPOINTMENT* with self or others.

6. *EMBARRASSMENT* leading to anger can be a cover story for shame, anxiety, or perfectionism.

7. *JEALOUSY* can really be a questioning of our own sense of value.

8. *HURT* feelings are often our "inner child" (see below) being triggered, leaving us feeling vulnerable.

9. Being *MISUNDERSTOOD* can be an indicator of not being seen as Who You Really Are.

10. *GUILT*

11. *SHAME*

12. *SENSORY OVERLOAD* is when we are overwhelmed by the five senses or by an onslaught of emotions, triggering excessive inner tension that explodes as anger.

ॐ

DEFUSE AND NEUTRALIZE OUR ANGER

We should always plan to recognize our anger precursor whenever we are about to blow or feel our anger rising. There are certain methods for releasing our inner stress.

Some of these are achievable by:

1. *MEDITATION or MINDFULNESS*
2. *BREATH-WORK*
3. *RELAXATION*
4. *REFRAMING OUR INTERNAL DIALOGUE* by recognizing truth instead of assumptions
5. We should try to express ourselves to others assertively, not aggressively.
6. We should be willing to acknowledge our true selves so that we know what we really need.
7. We should acknowledge that many of the above-mentioned feelings are leftovers from our upbringing. This is referred to be our "inner child," and it warns us about current events, but it does so from the powerlessness of childhood. We must remember that as adults, we have the power to address this circumstance maturely.
8. We should attempt singing, painting, or movement, such as exercise or dancing, to release our inner stress and innermost sentiments.
9. Rather than burying our emotions, we should express our frustrations and pains as they arise, while they are still tiny, bearable, and controllable so that we do not have to confront the erupting volcano.

> *"Holding on to anger is like grasping a hot coal with the intent of throwing it at someone else; you are the one who gets burned."*

IV

ARE WE CHASING RAINBOWS?

"We will continue to chase rainbows until we recognize that they are rainbows and there is no pot of gold at the end of them"

We humans have a tendency to constantly adapt to new situations. The euphoria fades. Rage soothes. Even the overwhelming power of sadness fades with time.

The ongoing drive to better ourselves and our circumstances, to seek a better life, or to pursue pleasure is what keeps our human race flourishing. However, it also places us on a hedonic treadmill in which we are continuously seeking the next great objective.

We create objectives and expectations such as obtaining the next major promotion, accomplishing a tough assignment, or completing a massive project. We rush for those things, frequently working hard and going to lengths to better ourselves, picturing how happy we would be when we reach this objective. But if we achieve or get at our objective, the emotion is more of a relief than euphoria.

We get a sense of closure on all the effort that led up to this moment. The happiness even if it does show up, is only momentary, often lasting a few hours, days or sometimes even a week.

Before we know it, we're back on the treadmill, pursuing the next big objective, a greater goal, a better responsibility, or anything else that will make us happy. We run again, set a new goal for ourselves, just to return to our baseline, our predetermined level of bliss.

೫

Broadly speaking, we experience two types of happiness in our life.

1. Hedonism

The pursuit of pleasure is referred to as hedonism. The phrase alludes to the immediate joy we get when we do something we enjoy or avoid doing something we dislike. Example: Food and Sex

2. Eudaimonia

Eudaimonia is the fulfillment we get from engaging in worthwhile activities such as assisting others or doing something to help ourselves grow.

Both hedonic and eudaimonic happiness promote the growth of endurance and the ability to recover from setbacks and losses. A phase of grieving is natural and necessary after a life event that has left us reeling from loss or grief.

Finding methods to experience both personal pleasure and purpose might therefore help us get closer to a new feeling of happiness, even if it doesn't feel precisely similar to the joy we felt before a severe loss.

৪৩

The answer to the question "Are we Happy?" may be answered using the "Hedonic treadmill," a psychological concept.

৪৩

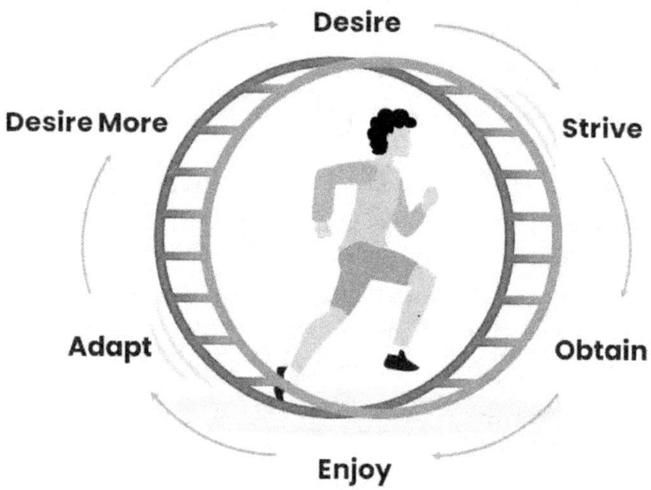

Hedonic Treadmill

It is a hypothesis that claims that no matter what occurs, people always revert to their baseline level of happiness. For example, if a person's income increases, so do his or her expectations and demands, resulting in no long-term increase in happiness. It lessens the emotional effect of occurrences.

Everyone has a happy "set point," where we retain a consistent degree of happiness throughout our lives, regardless of what happens around us. This theory is analogous to working on a treadmill considering that no matter how hard one strives to enhance happiness, one will remain in the same spot.

If we have a low set point, it suggests we are vulnerable to unhappiness or despair, and we should not be too hard on ourselves. Whatever our starting place, there is always room for progress. Our actions, beliefs, and attitudes all have an impact.

"According to Lyubomirsky's research, genetics determine 50% of our happiness, external influences determine 10%, and the other 40% is up to us to control. As a result, we have some power over our own happiness."

ॐ

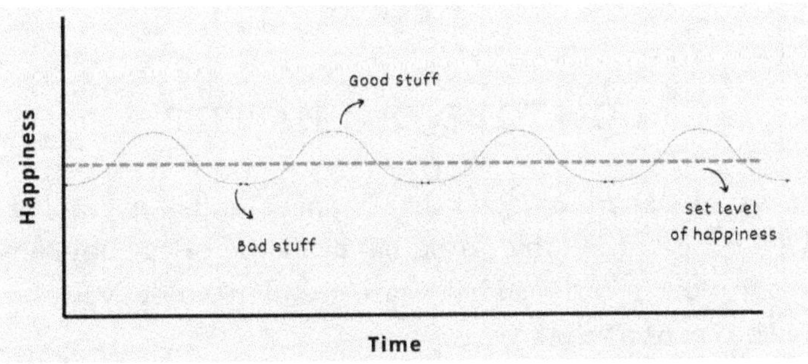

Even though it appears to us that no matter what we do, long-term happiness is not achievable. We must never forget,

1. The set point is not neutral

Even if we adjust and return to a prior position, the shift is beneficial rather than neutral.

2. The set point is individualized

Everyone has a different set point, and it varies greatly from person to person.

3. We have multiple set points.

The core premise is that various types of happiness might go in opposite directions at the same time.

4. Happiness can change

A long-term shift in our happiness level is possible.

5. Individual differences in adaptation

Each of us adapts at a different rate and to a different extent. Individuals who are happy analyze experiences in a positive and useful manner. Unhappy people tend to focus on the bad parts of events, find flaws in great occurrences, or reflect on how things used to be better.

HOW TO BECOME HAPPIER

If we take anything good that happens to us for granted, we will never be able to be happy. Some of the Tal-Ben-suggestions mentioned below are useful in our daily lives.

1. Try to be human

We must acknowledge our feelings, which include fear, grief, and worry. Rejecting them leads to disappointment.

2. Simplify your life

We should aim to limit multitasking and focus on one activity at a time.

3. Find meaning and pleasure

Instead of doing what we feel forced to do, we should endeavor to participate in goals that we truly want to attain. Spending time with our hobbies and loved ones may be really beneficial.

4. Focus on the positive and be grateful

5. We should put more effort into our relationships, whether with our spouse or with our family.

6. We should practice meditation, yoga, and breathing techniques. Exercising also leads to decreased levels of depression.

To boost our happiness, we should think about what we actually want to accomplish, pick people and activities we like, learn by revisiting our negative ideas, and concentrate on the current now.

V

HORMONAL COCKTAIL

"Love is indeed, at root, the product of firing of neurons and release of hormones"

We feel better by socializing with our friends or loved ones. An hour of unanticipated traffic delays may sadden our mood. However, our mood is more complex than the circumstances and surroundings we experience. It's important for us to consider brain chemistry as well.

Neurotransmitters and hormones are substances that help our brain comprehend, assess, and express our feelings between the moment we become aware of a situation and the time we respond to it. Each neurotransmitter and hormone has a unique purpose; when it is active, it conveys a certain emotion and stimulates a specific portion of the brain.

The primary signaling molecules, particularly when it comes to happiness, are:

Serotonin, Dopamine, Endorphins & Oxytocin

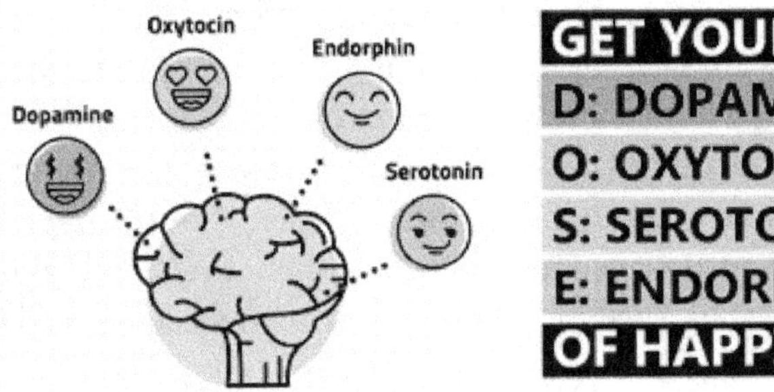

We may take proactive steps to naturally boost the levels of these happy chemicals in our bodies and brains by being conscious of their importance in our bodies and brains and their influence on our mental health. So having joyful hormones would make us happy!

Hormones are principally generated by several glands in the human body to increase communication between two glands or between a gland and an organ.

Our body's hormone levels fluctuate throughout the day. A cortisol spike, for example, wakes us up in the morning, whereas melatonin, another hormone, helps us prepare for bed in the evening. Hormones inform us if we are hungry, full, happy, or unhappy.

The endocrine system, a distinct physiological system, regulates the generation and release of hormones into circulation. It is a system of glands that covers the entire body and is regulated by the pituitary gland in the brain. Each gland produces at least one hormone.

Certain hormones influence mood, pleasure, kinship, and even pain relief. But that's not all. These compounds are necessary for human health, metabolism, reproduction, and growth and development.

Neurotransmitters are another name for these hormones. Except for where they act, hormones and neurotransmitters are nearly identical.

Happy hormones may be found in a variety of organs and tissues throughout the body, but happy neurotransmitters can only be found in the brain and central nervous system, where they can interact directly with neurons.

The body produces a variety of feel-good chemicals that boost mood and promote general well-being. Some can reduce anxiety and prevent depressive symptoms, while others can produce pleasure, joy, connection, and trust. These are the most pleasant compounds in our bodies.

Less well recognized is that our environment, relationships, nutrition, exercise routine, and, in some circumstances, even our gut microorganisms may all influence our levels of happy hormones. It is true that the decisions you make on a daily basis can influence how you feel.

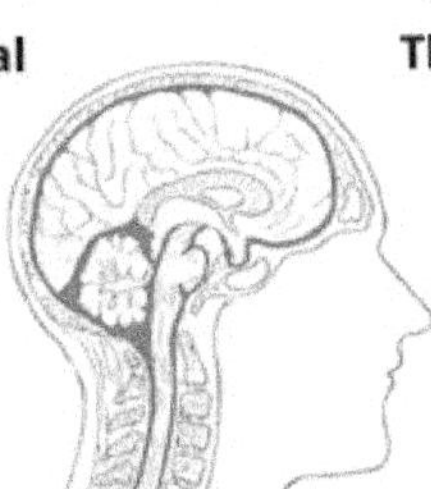
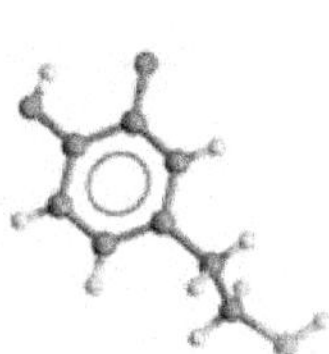

DOPAMINE
The Reward Chemical

- Eating Food
- Achieving a Goal
- Complete a Task
- Self-Care Activities

OXYTOCIN
The Love Hormone

- Socialising
- Physical Touch
- Petting Animals
- Helping Others

ENDORPHIN
The Painkiller

- Exercising
- Listening to Music
- Watch a Movie
- Laughter

SEROTONIN
The Mood Stabilizers

- Sun Exposure
- Mindfullness
- Be with Nature
- Meditation

Let us see how we can get our daily DOSE of Happiness:

DOPAMINE

Dopamine is a unique hormone that makes us joyful while also keeping us attentive and aware. The dopamine system is involved in several processes and has been linked to a number of severe illnesses. The following are some of the systems with which it communicates:

- motor control and cognitive function
- the brain's motivation and reward system
- decision-making and impulse control
- memory and attention
- maternal and reproductive behaviors

This molecule is a component of the brain's reward system, which is responsible for making you feel good and motivating you to seek out more. Dopamine is naturally released before you ingest anything you believe it is because of food or during sex. It is thought to be the system's motivating factor.

ॐ

OXYTOCIN

Oxytocin is a hormone that encourages trust and intimate bonds. It is particularly active during labor because it causes contractions. It also has an important but lesser-known role as a neurotransmitter in modulating stress reactions and relaxing the neurological system.

It has been linked to compassion, trust, and human connection; however, some research suggests that it may also have a role in the success of some romantic relationships.

Higher blood levels of the oxytocin hormone have been related to stronger feelings of affection, caring, and appreciation in romantic relationships.

The brain constantly analyses our environment for hazards using our hearing, sight, taste, touch, and smell.

Oxytocin is created as a result of these signals. It is created under stressful situations to counteract the effects of cortisol, as well as in reaction to touch and even the correct amount of eye contact.

Oxytocin controls everything, including the immune system, pain perception, and healing. It prolongs life by boosting physical strength and wound healing.

If you're wondering how to release oxytocin, it's quite simple to accomplish. Since oxytocin is released when you connect with kind people and are surrounded by encouraging individuals, it's a good thing there isn't an oxytocin meal.

SEROTONIN

Serotonin, the "original happy hormone," is required for circadian rhythm, brain function, digestion, and sleep. Surprisingly, the stomach produces up to 90% of the serotonin in our bodies.

First, the enteric nervous system in the gut produces the hormone as a neurotransmitter, which interacts with the body's tissues as a hormone before being released into circulation.

Second, it has recently been discovered that our gut flora influences serotonin synthesis. Despite how strange it may sound, the zillions of microbes in our gut have the power to stimulate serotonin-producing cells.

Tryptophan is converted to serotonin in our intestines. It is an important amino acid that the body cannot generate and must thus be obtained from food.

It is general knowledge that a diet high in fiber-rich plant foods, moderate amounts of meat, and regular exercise may help improve one's spirit, relieve anxiety, and even battle depression.

Exercise has been demonstrated to increase levels of tryptophan and serotonin. It also increases the diversity of our gut flora, which is helpful to our general health.

Although serotonin cannot be consumed, there are two strategies to boost serotonin levels through food.

To begin, increase the number of prebiotic items in our diet to encourage the beneficial bacteria that make short-chain fatty acids.

Following food items can be consumed to increase serotonin levels.

1. Eggs
2. Cheese
3. Pineapple
4. Tofu
5. Salmon
6. Nuts and Seeds
7. Turkey

80

ENDORPHINS

Contrary to popular belief, endorphins do not always make us joyful. Endorphins, a kind of neurotransmitter, and hormones are both analgesics. They block pain signals from reaching the central nervous system by binding to opioid receptors, which the body naturally produces as morphine.

Endorphins and dopamine are frequently mistaken since they are both regarded to be happy-making compounds. Dopamine, the feel-good hormone, is released when endorphins attach to central nervous system receptors, therefore they are related in certain respects.

Nonetheless, happy endorphins gained appeal since they cause euphoria rather than suppressing pain signals. The well-known "runner's high" is indeed generated by a considerable surge of endorphins. Furthermore, the powerful combination of dopamine and endorphins explains why some people acquire a "running addiction."

৪৩

CONCLUSION

These hormones or neurotransmitters could also go by other names that are more familiar. They contribute to the development of a positive mindset and upbeat feelings. For instance, the hug hormone is oxytocin, the feel-good hormone is dopamine, and the happy hormone is serotonin.

The gut flora has a role in the production of neurotransmitters including dopamine and serotonin. These facilitate communication between neurons and connect the nervous system to the intestines. In other words, a happy stomach leads to a happy mind!

Our body may naturally increase our levels of dopamine, serotonin, and oxytocin, which can elevate our mood, emotions, and even cognitive function.

৪৩

Is it Happiness or Pleasure?

Dopamine, a neurotransmitter in the brain linked to rewards and motivation, differs significantly from serotonin, a hormone linked to happiness and deep satisfaction.

Dopamine, it turns out, affects parts of the brain quite differently than serotonin, which we know has a role in reducing anxiety and preventing depression. Serotonin is directly linked to happiness, making it one of the main components of many antidepressant medications.

At least 14 different receptors are impacted by serotonin, which then communicates feelings of happiness to various parts of the brain.

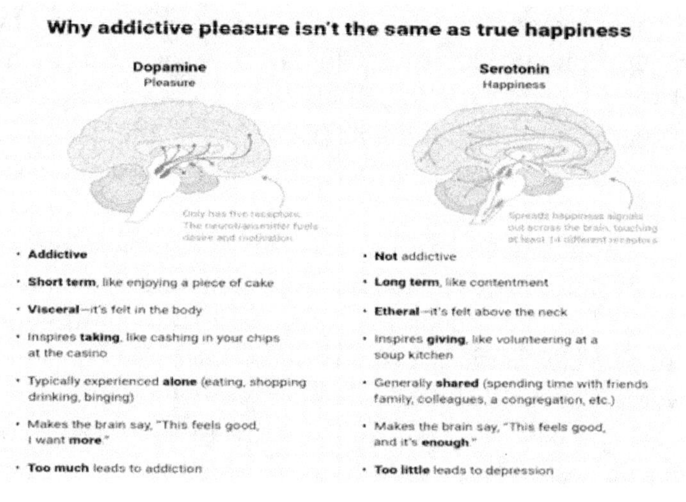

Serotonin and receptors in many parts of the brain combine to produce sensations of joy, love, and fulfillment. This is only one example of the many ways that happiness may be experienced.

Dopamine, on the other hand, only has five brain receptors. These receptors are activated by the neurotransmitter to provide pleasurable and motivating feelings. Dopamine controls a number of mental functions in our brains, such as motivation, pleasure, and rewards.

There is also some evidence that it contributes to normal hallucinations. Since it fuels a cycle of desire and reward, it will never make us entirely happy or content, making us feel like we have enough and are enough.

VI
AIN'T NO MOUNTAIN HIGH ENOUGH

"Believe you can and you're halfway there"

Confidence is something that we all deal with at times. We want to be confident in ourselves, yet those tiny self-doubt whispers appear anytime we want to put ourselves out there, take chances, or attempt something new.

They advise us to play it safe and do things the way we've always done them to avoid being hurt, embarrassed, or rejected, but we don't have to listen to them all of the time.

In fact, doing activities that our conscience thinks are dangerous or out of the ordinary is a terrific approach to boosting confidence.

Cultivating confidence is the first step toward good self-esteem and personal growth, but for most of us, it is difficult. To create confidence, we may need to do something we've never done before or think in a way we've never thought of before. This might be frightening, but cognitive restructuring and behavior modification are crucial components of many forms of effective therapy.

Here are eight suggestions to build confidence:

FACE A FEAR

Fear is frequently at the root of low self-esteem. When we're afraid of the outcome of anything, we do not approach it with confidence.

Until we confront our fear, it has authority over us and amplifies the voice of self-doubt.

Consider a fear you've confronted and how you felt afterward. You will feel free and proud and might even want to do the things you were terrified of.

When we make a commitment to do something that terrifies us every day, once a week, or once a month, we will see our confidence rise swiftly.

BEFRIEND FAILURE

We haven't tried until we've failed. To fully succeed, we must be willing to accept the chance of failure. The more mistakes we make, the more we will learn and improve. Accepting our mistakes will allow them to propel us forward.

Failure frequently appears to be the end of the road, yet it is usually only the beginning. Once we accept the initial disappointment, we will be more prepared to succeed the following time.

We will begin believing in ourselves and our talents by taking risks and being willing to fail.

⁗

DOUBT YOUR DOUBT

Doubt is the adversary of certainty. It holds us in suspense and, at times, even makes us skeptical. Instead of questioning ourselves, we should counterbalance it by questioning our doubts.

We should examine the reality of what our skepticism is telling us. Whenever any limiting beliefs occur, challenge them.

⁗

AFFIRM OWN STRENGTHS, TALENTS, AND ACCOMPLISHMENTS

People who lack confidence prefer to focus on their flaws rather than their virtues. Making a list of our abilities, talents, and achievements can build our confidence.

We should be honest with ourselves and remind ourselves of our excellence. We have a tendency to trust things that we are continuously exposed to. Our confidence is influenced tremendously by our daily thoughts, especially recurring thoughts.

Consistency is key to lasting change. If we want to be more confident, we should make a habit of reminding ourselves of our unique gifts and abilities.

⁗

EMBODY CONFIDENCE

We should Feel more confident if we want to be more confident.

When we are feeling scared and unsure, we should take a minute to close our eyes and remember a period when we were confident and self-assured.

By taking ourselves back to that time by using all of our senses, we'll be able to nurture that emotion in the current moment.

Working on our posture, and choosing a body stance that exudes confidence can take us a step forward in that direction.

℘

LISTEN TO EMPOWERING MUSIC

Music is excellent at eliciting emotions. Turning on some upbeat music can help whenever we want to feel more assured.

℘

SET A REALISTIC GOAL AND TAKE ACTION TO ACHIEVE IT

Our accomplishments significantly add to our sentiments of self-confidence. We will learn to trust ourselves and our talents more if we make a promise and follow through on it.

We frequently make extreme resolutions, such as New Year's resolutions, that need vast, sweeping change.

Then we don't follow them. Every year, those who exercise once a month try to exercise one hour every day and virtually always last about a week or two before giving up.

We lose trust and faith in our skills when we fail to follow through on a commitment we make to ourselves, and our confidence suffers as a result.

It takes a tremendous amount of time, work, and devotion to create new behaviors.

When setting new goals, we should try to be realistic and make sure that our goals are attainable. Starting slowly and setting small goals can help.

By following through with our commitments, no matter how small, we learn to trust ourselves and gain confidence in what we're capable of achieving.

ॐ

MAKE A DIFFERENCE

Do something to give back and contribute to society. Consider volunteering or making a donation to our favorite charity. Do something for someone else. It doesn't have to be a major contribution.

Doing something to help our community and society.

Volunteering or donating to one of our favorite charities.

Making an effort to help someone else would make us feel good. Realizing our genuine value as individuals will strengthen us and boost our self-esteem.

We may feel overwhelmed if we try to do too much at once. We should remember that confidence is a sense of trust that takes time to develop.

Thus, we must be patient with ourselves and recognize that the journey begins with a single step.

We should take baby steps and before we know it, we will arrive at our destination feeling confident and capable.

Confidence isn't a trait we're born with. Just like the muscles in our body, it's something we build and gets better at every day with continuous practice.

Knowing our beliefs and practicing positive thinking are two things that can help us create confidence in the long run.

VII

CONTROL YOUR PSYCHE

We all have unique personalities. We have both a positive and negative side. Our ability to balance both forms our entire identity.

Sigmund Freud's psychoanalytic theory may be used to explain the notion of psychoanalysis. Because everyone possesses unconscious thoughts, memories, feelings, and desires, he believes that therapy should be used to access the mind's hidden sentiments and experiences. Only then would the patient feel mental catharsis.

The human psyche comprises both positive and bad characteristics. The id, ego, and superego are three unique components of the mind that emerge at different stages of our lives These are neither physical nor mental components, but rather systems.

The ego is the real component of the mind that mediates between the wants of the id and the super-ego.

The id is the primal and instinctive part of the mind that contains sexual and aggressive urges as well as buried memories.

Even while each component of the personality consists of distinct traits, they work together to form a whole, and each component contributes in a relative way to how someone behaves.

INTERNAL DRIVE (ID)

The id is the instinctive and fundamental aspect of one's psyche. The libido, a type of basic physical desire utilized for anything from survival instincts to art appreciation, is a component of the id, an area of the unconscious that stores all urges and impulses.

It encompasses all of the genetic personality elements present at birth, including the sexual (life) instinct Eros (which contains the libido) and the violent (death) instinct Thanatos.

The id is the impulsive (and unconscious) component of the psyche that responds immediately to our most basic wants, needs, and desires. The id constitutes the totality of a newborn child's identity; the ego and super-ego emerge later.

Because it has no touch with the outer world, the id remains infantile throughout a person's life and does not mature with age or experience. The id operates in the mind's unconscious realm, where it is untouched by reality, logic, or the outer world.

The pleasure principle, which states that all desires should be satisfied immediately, is the foundation upon which the id operates. We sense pleasure when the id receives what it desires; when it doesn't, we feel "displeasure" or tension.

Primitive, illogical, irrational, and fantasy-focused primary process thinking is employed by the id. This type of process thinking is selfish and wishful in nature, with no grasp of objective reality.

ℬ

EGO

The ego is the part of the id that has been directly impacted by its surroundings. The ego is the only component of the conscious personality. It is what the individual is aware of while contemplating oneself, and it is what they usually try to present to others.

The ego develops to serve as a bridge between the id's perceptions and the outside real world. It is a personality characteristic associated with decision-making. The ego must be reasonable, but the id has to be chaotic and irrational.

The truth principle states that the ego seeks logical answers to the id's demands, usually sacrificing or postponing pleasure in order to avoid social penalties. Based on social reality, the ego determines how to act.

It focuses on devising a realistic strategy for having fun. The ego has no concept of good and wrong; something is only regarded wonderful if it accomplishes its goal without hurting the ego or the id.

If the ego fails in its attempt to employ the reality principle and anxiety occurs, unconscious defense mechanisms are deployed to help fight off unpleasant feelings (i.e., anxiety) or make good things appear better for the person.

The ego employs secondary process thinking, which is rational, practical, and concerned with problem-solving. If a line of action fails, it is reconsidered until an answer is found. This is known as reality testing, and it allows the person to rule their ego and demonstrate impulse control as well as self-discipline.

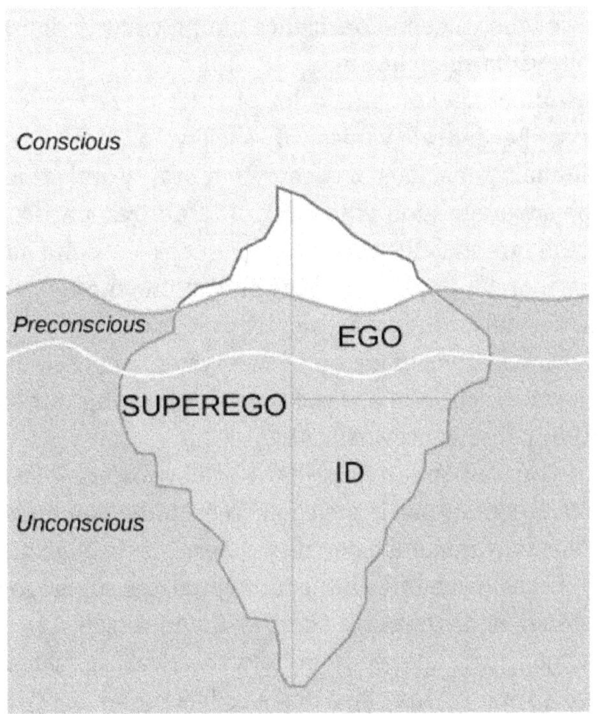

&

SUPER EGO

The superego integrates societal standards and values acquired from others and one's parents. Depending on which side (the ego-deal or conscious) is active, the superego is seen as the source of both rewards (a sense of pride and fulfillment) and penalties (feelings of shame and guilt).

The superego, a component of the unconscious, is the source of the voice of conscience (doing what is right) and the source of self-criticism.

The superego contains a lot of rules or restrictions. It reflects the moral values of society, and people are occasionally conscious of their own morality and ethics.

The superego's job is to control id desires, particularly those that are socially unacceptable, such as sex and hatred. Furthermore, it has the effect of persuading the ego to seek idealistic goals rather than merely practical ones.

The superego is made up of two systems: consciousness and the ideal self. When we do something wrong, our "inner voice," or conscience, warns us.

The conscience can punish the ego by fostering feelings of guilt. For example, if the ego agrees to the demands, the superego may make the person feel terrible through guilt.

By imposing shame on the individual, the superego may punish behavior that falls short of the ideal self. The ideal self, which the super-ego employs to reward us when we behave "properly," may also make us feel proud.

Guilt is a pretty common difficulty due to the id's impulses and drives and the superego's prohibitions and restrictions.

&

HEALTHY PSYCHE VS NEUROTIC PSYCHE

Healthy Psyche

Neurotic Psyche

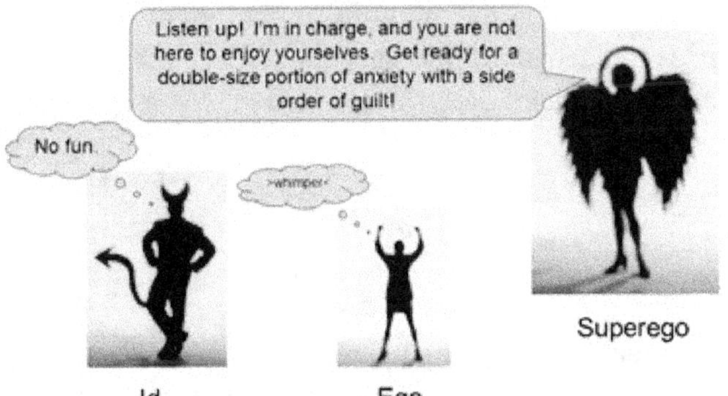

In order to maintain control over the id, the ego employs defense mechanisms, which are automatic, unconscious mental strategies or coping styles used to reduce anxiety or guilt associated with the situation, as well as to protect us from our own dangerous impulses, unacceptable behavior, and unpleasant thoughts or feelings.

It also aids in reducing the threat to our self-esteem posed by the demands of the superego and reality. There are many different defense mechanisms used by the ego.

Among the more common are:

Denial – refusing to accept reality

Rationalization – justifying behavior with a socially acceptable reason as opposed to the real reason

Sublimation – converting unacceptable behavior to a more acceptable form

Displacement – satisfying an impulse with a substitute

Projection – attributing undesired impulses, thoughts, or feelings, to others

Repression – blocking a painful memory or unacceptable impulse

Self-Hypnosis is a mind-full technique one could practice regularly to fulfill a set goal.

The best affirmation we can tell ourselves in Emile Coue's words,

"Every day in every way, I am getting better and better"

If this statement is repeatedly told to ourselves that we are confident, that we are a winner, and that people like us, then it would become true.

It works because once we unconsciously believe something, that belief is expressed in our body language and speech patterns so that other people would react to those signals.

By means of affirmations, we could overcome the primitive instinct thus favoring Ego and Super Ego which enables us to develop a calm state of mind reducing internal conflict.

The process called "mental rehearsal" can also prove to be very beneficial. It is a means by which we practice for an event in our mind over and over again prior to D-Day.

VIII

SELF ASSESSMENT

Dunning-Kruger Effect

The Dunning-Kruger effect happens when we overestimate our own ability due to a lack of information and abilities in a certain field. This impact, on the other hand, encourages us who succeed in a specific field to believe the work is straightforward for everyone and underestimate our own relative talents.

Because of the Dunning-Kruger effect, we may be unaware of our own skills because we believe that everyone else is similarly skilled at what we find straightforward. As a result, we lose the ability to distinguish our own distinct qualities and capabilities.

Furthermore, if we achieve something challenging for us, we may accidentally feel that it is our area of strength. In actuality, we can just be below-average performer who is now getting close to normal levels.

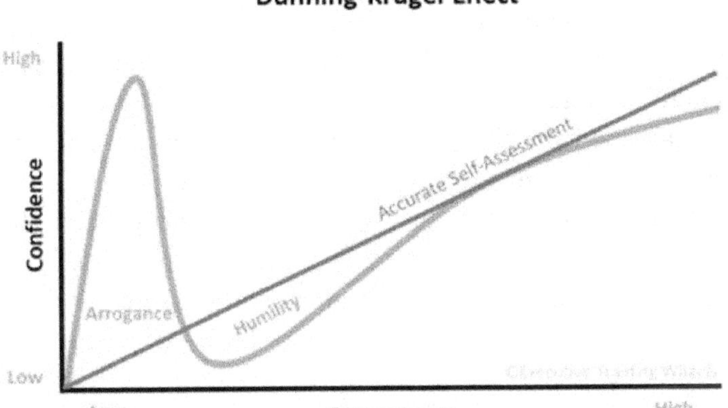

Dunning-Kruger Effect

As we can see, this distinction may have an impact on how we seek opportunities or work. We may question our friends and classmates about our skills. This choice was not made in error.

Knowing about the Dunning-Kruger effect may help us determine whether to depend on our own judgment and when to seek help from individuals who may evaluate us more objectively than we do.

We may also feel disappointed as a result of the effect when others do not recognize our apparent ability. We can be expecting a promotion, but it ends up going to someone who was surprised to be given the opportunity. It's likely that our mediocre performance caused us to feel we were doing well, while their expertise led them to believe they were doing great.

Because we feel we are great at something, we may pass up opportunities to learn from someone who is genuinely more talented or educated than us. Furthermore, feeling we are poor at something when we actually have exceptional expertise may restrict us from taking advantage of opportunities for teaching and knowledge-sharing.

As a consequence of their confidence, the best of the best remain behind closed doors, and as a society, we miss out on learning from them. People with below-average abilities are usually in the limelight.

Unfortunately, the most egocentric people are also the most ignorant. This has significant ramifications for our democracy since it suggests that our most illiterate folks are also our most confident. These dumb people are not only reluctant to learn since they believe they know everything, but they actively distribute erroneous information.

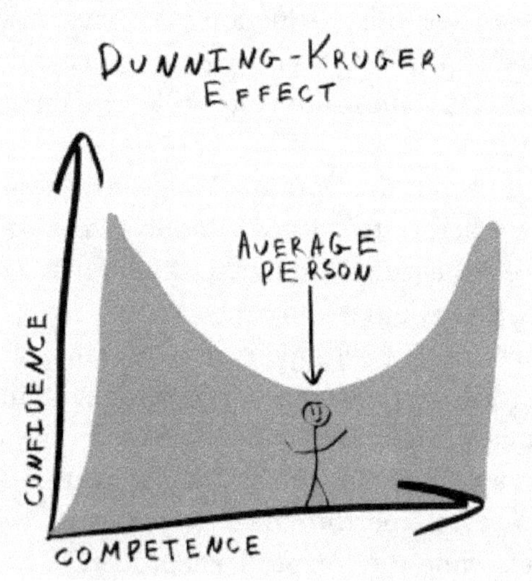

The Dunning-Kruger effect is primarily motivated by an abundance of misinformation rather than a scarcity of knowledge. We recognize when we are stupid, yet inaccurate information fools us into thinking we are knowledgeable experts, leading us to carelessly click the "share" button.

This influence has detrimental consequences that have previously been recognized on a national or worldwide scale. In essence, having a less educated audience may be good if we are a politician. People who know less about political and global issues are more likely to agree with us, believe they are well-informed, vote, and communicate their views to others.

Those in the upper to the middle of the pack who are slightly aware of political concerns are more likely to disengage from political debate and avoid voting because they do not regard themselves as worthwhile participants. Even though professionals, who are the most informed of all, are conscious of their vast knowledge, they avoid educating the general people because they are ignorant of how unusual their experience is.

Because of our culture's self-awareness issue, illiterate or uneducated people may boldly seize the microphone while experts and knowledgeable people sit behind the stage, drawing back the curtains. This phenomenon spreads erroneous information and ill-informed viewpoints throughout our social contexts, preventing us from benefiting from actual learning opportunities from one another.

"If too many foolish people believe they are the greatest, our civilization will devolve into a swarm of maturing fish in a small, narrowing pond."

ॐ

Why does it happen?

People with a limited understanding of a subject are unable to notice their own mistakes or knowledge gaps. These blind spots keep individuals from seeing where they're going wrong, enabling them to assume they're doing well.

Instead, individuals at the pinnacle of their profession are unable to recognize their area of competence since it comes so naturally to them that they are oblivious that it does not work this way for everyone. They are unaware that some may find the assignment more challenging because of how quickly they acquire particular talents or knowledge areas.

They overestimate everyone else's abilities while underestimating their own.

Financial expertise, political understanding, chess, driving, and even medical knowledge have all been shown to have an influence.

ॐ

Why it is important

The Dunning-Kruger effect is critical because it makes us aware of our own blind spots and allows us to adjust how we view ourselves. It takes a step back to see that your own self-assessments are biased and likely incorrect because it is nearly imperceptible to those who are experiencing them.

If we are making judgments only on our own skills and talents, we have most likely not examined enough reliable information.

Furthermore, relying exclusively on another person's appraisal of their talents distorts your knowledge. By allowing someone to persuade us that they are deserving of our patronage or a promotion just because they feel they are performing very well, we may be completely misinformed and they will be grossly inflating their own skills.

The Dunning-Kruger effect may cause us to favor charismatic people over trustworthy ones. This has a significant influence on society because we tend to listen to those who speak up first and loudest, rather than those whose ideas carry the most weight.

Furthermore, understanding the Dunning-Kruger effect may reduce our jealousy of those who appear to "have it all together." The belief that we know everything is a warning sign that we lack knowledge.

"*I am not young enough to know everything.*"

How to avoid it

We may avoid being ignorant of our own performance by paying attention to and comprehending the performances of others. Our reaction may have alerted our friend, who only spoke a few words of Spanish, that he isn't as fluent as he thought. He had questioned how your classes were doing. Furthermore, his poor pronunciation might suggest that you have a secret ability for languages.

Simply being aware of the Dunning-Kruger effect may help us mitigate its effects. It's crucial to remember that if we think we're terrible at something, we're usually in the middle of the pack since it means we have enough perspective to notice our own flaws. But bear in mind: new levels mean new monsters.

We should keep in mind that even if we feel we are exceptional at something, we probably still have a lot to learn.

It is also possible to prevent the Dunning-Kruger effect by being open to criticism; however, this is certainly easier said than done. Low achievers typically do not respond well to criticism and have a continuous lack of ambition to improve.

If we receive feedback or constructive criticism, we shouldn't dismiss it; rather, chalk it up to ignorance on our part and use it to further our objectives.

"When arguing with a fool, first make sure the other person isn't doing the same thing."

IX

WHAT DO WE REALLY NEED?

"*Let yourself be drawn by the stronger pull of that which you truly love*"

Maslow's hierarchy of needs is a psychological motivational theory that consists of a five-tier model of human desires, typically represented as hierarchical levels within a pyramid.

The following necessities are given in order: physiological (food and clothing), safety (job security), love and belonging (friendship), esteem, and self-actualization.

Lower-level needs must be answered before higher-level demands may be addressed.

Deficiency needs vs. Growth needs

This five-stage strategy is divided into two sections: deficiency needs and growth needs. The first four levels are referred to as deficiency needs (D-needs), whereas the highest level is referred to as growth or being requirements (B-needs).

Deficiency needs arise as a result of deprivation and are thought to motivate people when unsatisfied. Furthermore, the need to satisfy such desires gets stronger the longer they go unsatisfied. For example, the longer a person goes without eating, the more hungry they will become.

When a deficit need is fulfilled, our efforts are typically focused toward meeting the next set of needs that we have yet to meet. These then become our most urgent needs. However, once resolved, growth demands continue to be felt and may even accelerate.

Growth needs stem from a desire to grow as a person, not from a lack of something. When these growth demands are addressed successfully, one may be able to attain the highest level of self-actualization.

Everyone is capable and wants to climb the ladder to self-actualization. Unfortunately, ignoring lower-level demands typically stifles progress. Life events such as divorce and job loss might cause an individual to move up or down the hierarchy.

As a result, not everyone will follow the hierarchy in the same order, but will instead cycle between different types of requests.

↾

FIVE-STAGES OF PYRAMID OF NEEDS

According to Maslow, individuals are motivated to satisfy certain desires, and certain needs take precedence over others.

Our most basic need is for physiological survival, and this will guide our actions. When we achieve that level, the level above us encourages us, and so on.

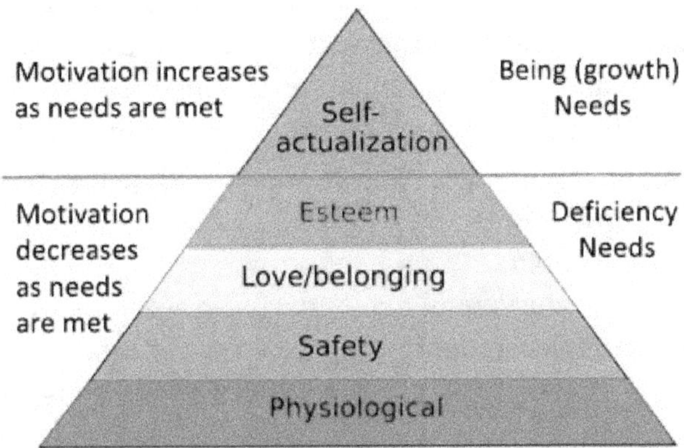

1. Physiological demands include air, food, water, shelter, clothing, warmth, sex, and sleep.

The human body cannot function properly unless these requirements are satisfied. Maslow considered physiological needs to be the most important, since if these are not met, all other needs become secondary.

2. Security and safety demands

After a person's physiological demands are addressed, the need for security and safety emerges. In their daily lives, people seek order, predictability, and control. The family and society can meet these criteria (e.g. police, schools, business and medical care).

Examples include emotional security, financial security (e.g., a job or social welfare), law and order, fearlessness, social stability, property, health and well-being (e.g. safety against accidents and injury).

3. Love and belongingness requirements -

Following the satisfaction of physiological and safety requirements, the third level of human wants is social, which includes emotions of belonging. Belonging is an emotional desire for interpersonal relationships, affiliation, proximity, and group participation in humans.

Belongingness demands include friendship, intimacy, trust, and acceptance, as well as receiving and giving affection and love.

4. Esteem needs

Maslow's hierarchy of needs places self-worth, accomplishment, and respect at the fourth level. Maslow classified esteem needs into two categories: self-esteem (dignity, achievement, mastery, independence) and regard for others (reputation or respect).

Maslow believes that the need for respect or reputation is the most important for children and adolescents, coming before true self-esteem or dignity.

5. Individualization

Maslow's hierarchy of needs is the highest level, and it corresponds to a person's potential, self-fulfillment, personal advancement, and peak experiences. Maslow defines this level as the desire to achieve all imaginable, to be the best that one can be.

Individuals may feel or focus intensely on this impulse. One individual, for example, may have a strong desire to become the ideal parent. In another case, the ambition may present itself monetarily, academically, or athletically. Others may express it via paintings, sketches, or inventions.

Maslow suggested a hierarchy of human needs, with the order of need changing based on external conditions or individual qualities. For example, he finds that for some people, the need for self-esteem is more important than the desire for love. Others' need for creative fulfilment may transcend even their most basic needs.

ॐ

THE EXPANDED HIERARCHY OF NEEDS

The following changes to the original five-stage model are underlined in the eight-stage model:

1. Biological and physiological requirements - air, food, water, shelter, warmth, sex, sleep, and so on.

2. Safety requirements: protection from the elements, security, order, law, stability, and fearlessness.

3. Needs for love and belonging - companionship, closeness, trust, and acceptance, as well as receiving and giving affection and love. Affiliation, belonging to a group (family, friends, work).

4. Esteem requirements These are divided into two categories: (i) esteem for oneself (dignity, success, mastery, independence) and (ii) the desire to be accepted and respected by others (e.g., status, prestige).

5. Cognitive needs: knowledge and comprehension, curiosity, investigation, a desire for meaning, and predictability.

6. Aesthetic needs - appreciation and pursuit of beauty, balance, shape, and so on.

7. Needs for self-actualization - attaining human potential, self-fulfillment, personal progress, and peak experiences. A strong desire to "become whatever one is capable of being" (Maslow, 1987, p. 64).

8. Transcendence requirements - A person is driven by ideals that go beyond the own self (e.g., mystical experiences and certain experiences with nature, aesthetic experiences, sexual experiences, service to others, the pursuit of science, religious faith, etc.)

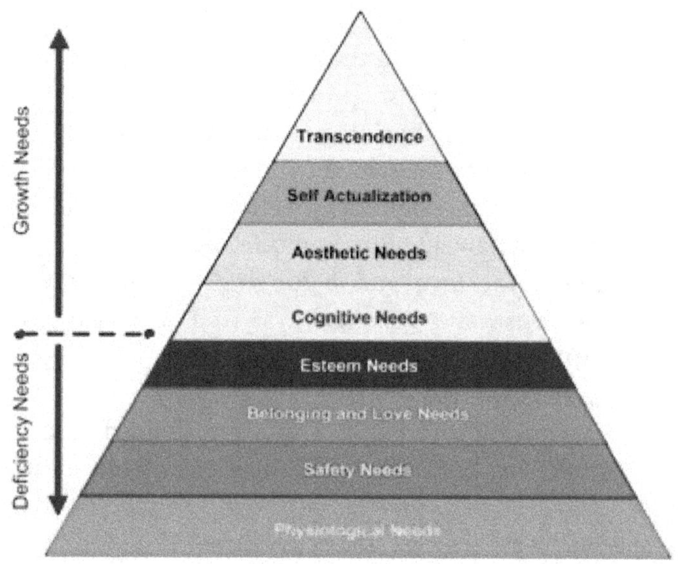

જી

SELF-ACTUALIZATION

Maslow established a more positive model of human behaviour that focuses on what goes right rather than psychopathology and what goes wrong with individuals. He was intrigued by our potential and how we manifest it.

According to Maslow, human motivation is based on people seeking fulfilment and change via personal growth. Individuals who have realised their entire potential are self-actualized.

Self-actualization development refers to the desire for personal progress and discovery that exists throughout a person's life. A human, according to Maslow, is always 'becoming' and is never stagnant in these terms. When a person identifies a meaningful purpose in life that is important to them, they have reached self-actualization.

Because each individual is unique, self-actualization motivation may take many different shapes.

Self-actualization can be realised for some through the creation of works of art or literature; for others, it might be realised through athletics, the classroom, or within a corporate setting.

Self-Actualization refers to a person's desire for self-fulfillment, namely his inclination to become actualized in who he is.

୨୦

CHARACTERISTICS OF SELF-ACTUALIZED PEOPLE

Although we are all theoretically capable of self-actualization, the vast majority of us will not, or will do so only to a limited level.

He was especially intrigued by the characteristics of people who, in his eyes, had reached their full potential as persons.

Maslow identified 15 characteristics of a self-actualized person after studying 18 people he considered to be self-actualized (including Abraham Lincoln and Albert Einstein).

Characteristics of self-actualizers:

1. They perceive reality efficiently and can tolerate uncertainty;
2. Accept themselves and others for who they are;
3. Be spontaneous in thought and action;
4. Problem-centered (not self-centered);
5. Unusual sense of humour;
6. Able to look at life objectively;
7. Highly creative;
8. Resistant to enculturation, but not purposefully unconventional;
9. Concerned for the welfare of humanity;
10. Capable of profound appreciation for fundamental life events;
11. Establish deep rewarding interpersonal ties with a few individuals;
12. Peak experiences;
13. Privacy needs;
14. Democratic views
15. High moral and ethical standards.

৪৩

HOW TO BECOME SELF-ACTUALIZED

- Experiencing life as a child, with full absorption and concentration;
- Trying new things rather than sticking to safe paths;
- Listening to our own feelings in evaluating experiences rather than the voice of tradition, authority, or the majority;
- Avoiding pretense ('game playing') and being honest;
- Being prepared to be unpopular if our views differ from those of the majority;
- Taking responsibility and working hard;
- Trying to identify our defenses and having the courage to give them up.

APPLICABILITY

A tired and hungry student, for example, will struggle to concentrate on studying. Students must feel emotionally and physically comfortable and accepted in the classroom in order to flourish and attain their full potential.

According to Maslow, a humanistic educational technique will produce individuals who are "They would be stronger, healthier, and would take more control of their own lives. People would begin to actively alter the society in which they lived if they had more personal accountability for their own lives and a realistic set of values to guide their choices ".

X
THE ART OF RETENTION

THE FORGETTING CURVE

When we're attempting to master a new skill or recall important knowledge, forgetting might be really unpleasant. If we can't recollect the information we need, our stress level will rise and our confidence will suffer. Worse, it may result in lost time, missed opportunities, and costly blunders.

To prevent forgetting and ensure that what we learn is kept, we must first understand why we forget.

Hermann Ebbinghaus, a German psychologist, was interested in understanding why we forget things and how to prevent them. As a consequence of his study, he created the Forgetting Curve, a graphic depiction of how gained knowledge deteriorates over time.

Ebbinghaus put his memory to the test by having himself recollect a list of fake syllables after varied periods of time. His observations and discoveries emphasized numerous important aspects of memory, including:

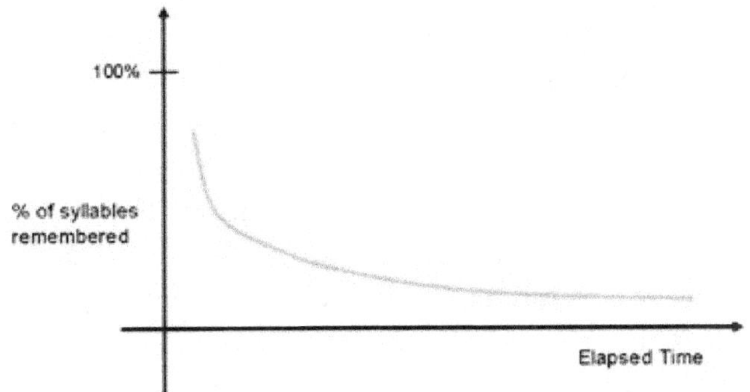

Ebbinghaus's forgetting curve

1. Memory deteriorates over time. We recall less and less new knowledge as the hours, days, and weeks pass if we don't try to relearn it once we learn it.
2. Following learning, there is a rapid decline in retention. The Forgetting Curve's precipitous decline at its beginning serves as a reflection of this.
3. Our capacity to retain knowledge declines without evaluation or reinforcement. For instance, we could leave a webinar or meeting with our brain filled with novel data and numbers, only to discover hours later that we can only vaguely recall it.
4. When something has meaning, it is simpler to remember it. The Forgetting Curve is most closely

matched by things that are meaningless or unimportant (like the gibberish syllables Ebbinghaus attempted to memorize). Therefore, if we're listening to a discussion on a topic we don't really understand or aren't very interested in, we'll probably forget it more quickly than if it were on a topic we thought to be incredibly interesting or thrilling.

5. Learning is impacted by the presentation of information. Depending on how effectively it is delivered, the identical piece of facts might be rendered more or less remembered. we'll probably have an easier time remembering information that has been presented simply and rationally. However, we might forget about that illegible, scrawled grocery list

6. Our memory is influenced by how we're feeling. Ebbinghaus thought that our ability to recall knowledge is significantly influenced by physiological conditions like stress and sleep. Many individuals see this as a vicious cycle in which stress makes it more difficult to recall, which in turn leads to additional stress. Additionally, there is compelling evidence that sleep may aid in the organization and storage of knowledge in our brains.

ॐ

Our ability to recall information is critical to our survival. Our brains are skilled at storing information that protects us against psychological or physical harm.

We are very good at remembering knowledge that is critical to our survival and that we must know. For example, things to avoid, routes or locations to take, and key persons in our lives. Furthermore, we typically keep memories of situations that entail powerful emotions such as surprise, fear, success, or relief for a longer period of time.

However, most of the material we want to learn — or that others rely on us to know — fades from memory much too rapidly.

Methods to enhance learning and retain knowledge

ಋ

Use "Spaced Learning"

The most important discovery Ebbinghaus made was that by reviewing new material at crucial places on the Forgetting Curve, we may slow down the rate at which we forget it. This approach is often referred to as "distributive practice" or "spaced learning."

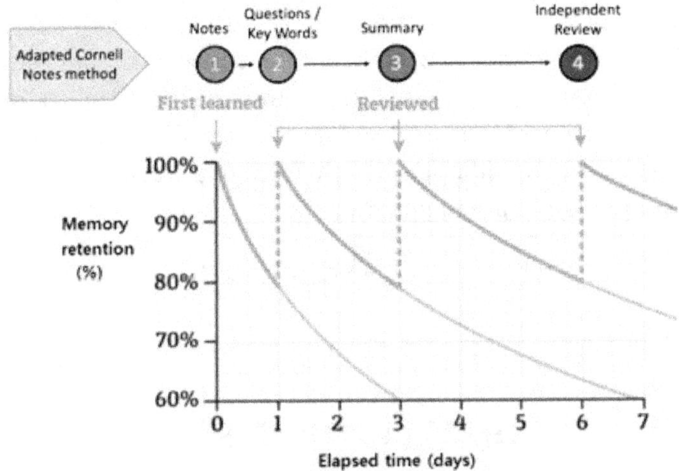

Spaced Learning

ಋ

Overlearn

Ebbinghaus also investigated "overlearning," or putting in more effort than is normally necessary for learning something. He realized that by doing so, he could improve retention and reduce the abrupt fall in memory.

He also mentioned that by adopting specific memory strategies, we may be able to recall even tough stuff.

୫୨

Make Information Meaningful

As we get a better comprehension of the information, our ability to recall it will increase. To encourage enhanced memory representation, Ebbinghaus advises using mnemonic procedures, which are systematic approaches for increasing memorization and memory.

Mnemonic tactics are not a new concept; the ancient Greeks and Romans used them to practice the "Art of Memory," since it was critical for orators to remember what they had to say while speaking in front of a crowd. Memory champions still use them now.

୫୨

୫୨

THE LEARNING CURVE

The learning curve was defined by Arthur Bills as a graphical tool for visualizing the rate of improvement in terms of a certain efficiency criterion as a result of practice.

A learning curve is a direct percentage on a graph that represents the relationship between a learner's success on a task and the number of attempts or time necessary to accomplish the activity.

According to the learning curve idea, a learner's efficiency in a task improves with time as the learner does the job more frequently.

A learning curve is a graphical depiction of the relationship between a person's skill level and their level of experience. Proficiency (measured on the vertical axis) often rises with experience (measured on the horizontal axis), which means that the more someone, groups, organizations, or industries undertake work, the higher our performance at the task.

The learning curve is the relationship between a learner's performance on a task or activity and the number of attempts or time necessary to finish the task.

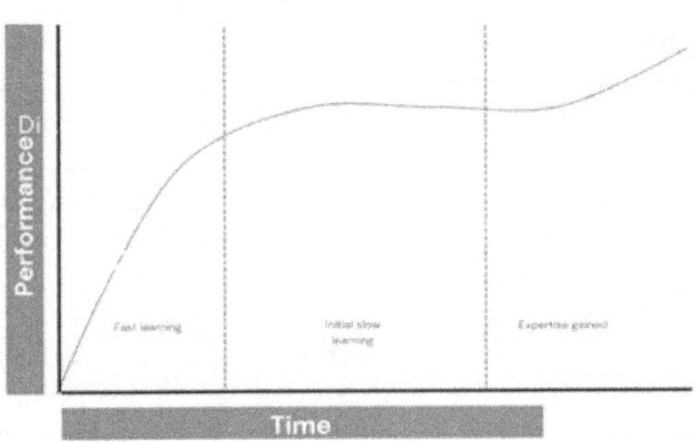

Advantages

Improve our comprehension - Comparing different learning curves helps us better grasp our understanding of a certain activity, allowing us to modify it properly.

The learning curve makes it easier to develop strategic initiatives to boost production.

Create a learning culture - The learning curve motivates us by establishing a culture of continual learning and learning assessment.

Making decisions - The learning curve aids in identifying trends that may be utilized to make sound decisions.

ॐ

Tips to flatten the learning curve

Specify our output unit.

Set measurable long-term and short-term goals to evaluate our performance and the effectiveness of our learning. we may clearly convey the goal of our learning program by describing what tasks we should be able to do by the conclusion of the learning.

Effective Learning

Make an effort to create an effective learning strategy. The right knowledge, guidance, and resources may make our learning curve more efficient and, in the long run, substantially shorter.

Individualized instruction

Create customized learning programs with learning content tailored to our learning style. With tailored learning, our engagement will rise, our learning efficacy will increase, and our learning curve will be shortened.

Make knowledgeable choices

If the data from the learning curve suggests that the current strategy is unsuccessful, look into alternate learning strategies and make additional modifications to improve our learning programmes. Finding the best strategy for improving performance may need several cycles of trial and error.

Coaching from mentors

No matter how well-designed and structured our learning programme is, it will usually fall short of providing we with all of the knowledge and information we need to do our work effectively. Receiving practical coaching from an experienced specialist can help we acquire new facts rapidly in this situation.

Constant observation

The learning curve should be monitored all year rather than only at times of change or when learning obstacles arise. Continuous monitoring detects problems as they develop, allowing we to immediately respond and alter our plan as needed.

XI

REINVIGORATING THE CREATIVE PROCESS

> *"When learning is purposeful, creativity blossoms.*
> *When creativity blossoms, thinking emanates.*
> *When thinking emanates, knowledge is fully lit.*
> *When knowledge is lit, economy flourishes"*

Graham Wallace, a social psychologist, initially outlined the creative process in his book "The Art of Thought," which was released in 1926, and most creators still adhere to it today.

Finding the right attitude might be difficult when it comes to being creative, whether via art, music, writing, or idea development. There are no fixed rules for creation. However, people go through five unconscious stages when being creative, and understanding these stages can help us arrange our time and get the most out of our ideas.

We commonly slip into the anguish of self-doubt and unhappiness as we proceed through the creative process, following the first exhilaration of a novel activity, thinking about the unlimited possibilities of creating a new song or building an online course. We are constantly discouraged and want to give up. After some time, an unexpected illumination happens, and appropriate concepts arise.

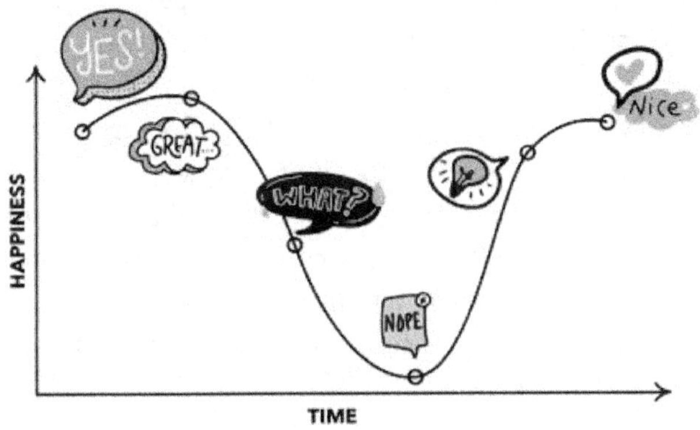

Although it appears disorganized on the surface, creativity follows certain basic rules. The nicest aspect is that we do not have to go through "down" time. Understanding the creative process will allow us to enjoy the entire experience by riding the wave rather than fighting it.

The creative mind, like every other mental function, is a muscle. Use it in little doses every day to build it. As humans, we are all capable of being creative; for example, whether we solve a problem, take a photograph, play the guitar, or start a business, we are using our creative minds.

"You can't use up creativity. The more you use, the more you have."

When we engage in creative activities on a regular basis, the creative process gets easier. It is preferable to prioritize quantity above quality. Why? Because repetition is necessary for the development of automatisms and the mastery of a skill. Furthermore, by experimenting and trying new ideas, we will learn to be less attached to the consequences of our work, which will free us from self-doubt and the fear of being evaluated, allowing us to take detours and increase our capacity to think creatively.

On the other hand, the concept that it takes 10,000 hours of labor to perfect anything is completely untrue. Regular practice is required along with making mistakes. As we gain information, analyzing them and making adjustments is how we truly progress.

"What you do every day matters more than what you do once in a while."

Let us now examine the five stages of creativity and how to avoid the agonizing period of doubt and dissatisfaction.

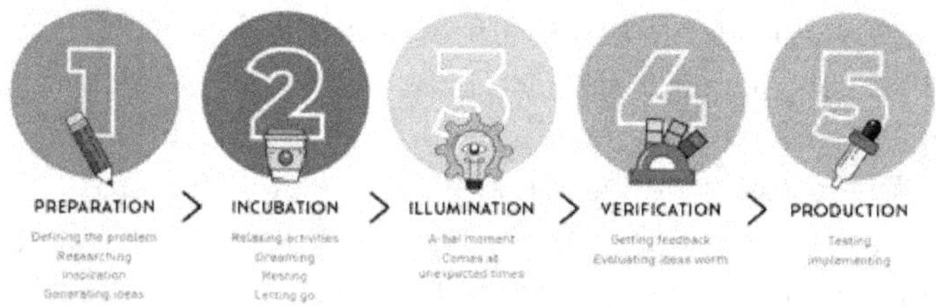

ॐ

Stage 1: Preparation

The brainstorming stage is the first stage. Allowing our thoughts to wander and uncovering inspiration might help us sow the seeds for our creative ideas. our sources of inspiration might be as specific as examining the works of writers or artists we admire, or as abstract as just watching our surroundings. You obtain the knowledge we need here to put our views together.

Find an area where there are no distractions and unwind.

The word "No" is not allowed within that space.

When we're still in the planning stage of concept development, it's helpful to explore and experiment without eliminating any ideas. We can simply have fun and write down all of our ideas, including the "bad" ones, to keep our mind from being caught on them.

Motivate ourselves to study everything we can. Allow ourselves some time to acquire acquainted with a wide range of books, music, and art.

"Everything you can imagine is real"

ॐ

Stage 2: Incubation

The second phase in the creative process is leaving all of our brainstormings behind, which may look unproductive at first. When we shift our focus to anything else, our subconscious continues to incorporate all of the acquired material into our new thinking.

1. Recognize our frustration and keep negative self-talk to a minimum.

It's possible that most individuals choose to skip this step. We expend excessive effort because we feel that if we stop, our momentum will also cease. When we begin to feel as though self-doubt is holding us back, this is an indication that we need a break.

Remember that, contrary to popular belief, our brain requires rest since it acts like a muscle. Agony ensues if ywe exert too much effort; nothing appears to work, we feel useless, and our motivation wanes.

2. Let go!

Creativity requires time, space, and solitude to assimilate new information, test ideas, and allow the subconscious to release its pattern recognition abilities. Significant intervals of idleness are required to encourage creativity.

It is what it is: unconscious processing. It happens when we set aside the problem we're trying to solve and give our subconscious an opportunity to address it. This explains why we usually have our best ideas when attempting to sleep.

3. Dream

Cutting back on sleep is bad for creativity since our brain needs a regular amount of sleep and daydreaming.

⮞⮜

Stage 3: Illumination

The Eureka! moment is the most enjoyable aspect of the process for everyone. Our solution or thought will have come from our subconscious now that we've arrived at this phase.
As in the case of Archimedes, this may not be a major event. We could have an idea while driving, cooking, or simply sitting idly. We could discover the lyrics to our next song verse, the ending to our book, or the answer to our present difficulty all of a sudden.

It's an "a-ha!" moment when we suddenly realize the answer. Most of us wrongly assume this to be creativity, although it is only a small part of the process.

Some tips:

1. Practice a low-level activity
2. Practice a calming activity to improve insights, such as yoga, meditation, taking a bath, or walking.
3. Change scenery
4. Go outside and enjoy nature or switch things up by working from a café or coworking space. Changing our surroundings also has an impact on our creative process.

છ

Stage 4: Verification

Following the formation of the original idea, this step entails critically analyzing the new idea and comparing it to various options.

To determine whether the offered remedy genuinely addresses the problem, compare it to the original issue, seek peer review, or do a marketing analysis. If the idea holds up after this step, we will either proceed with confidence or return to phases one and two.

But we shouldn't be concerned! Every thought will not be fantastic, but that does not mean the one following it will be.

Asking our peers for their opinions.

Choose people who will offer constructive criticism rather than ripping us apart with harsh comments. Our aim is to find an idea worth pursuing.

Stage 5: Production

At the end of the method, we bring our concept to life. We really write our story, paint our image, or invent something new here. Finally, we are ready to present our innovative idea to the rest of the world.

Begin implementation and Testing

It's at this point that the insights are formed into something valuable.

What to do when you encounter a "Creative Block"?

Sometimes we are stuck on a blank page and are out of ideas. We've all had creative blocks, whether we're graphic designers who create visual content on a daily basis or biology students writing lab reports for class. Fighting it and stressing about it typically makes things worse. Below is a list of suggestions to help break through any mental obstacles with an effective burst of creativity.

1. Look for inspiration from others.

When ideas are refined and improved upon, the most creative thinking occurs. Although it may not appear to be as creative, there is nothing wrong with initially seeking inspiration from others.

2. Constantly explore fresh ideas.

Though it may appear simple, write down any thought that occurs to mind on a blank sheet of paper. Even if the thought looks absurd and unimportant, writing it down may stimulate our imagination.

3. Create a checklist on a regular basis.

Many of my creative ideas come to us when we least expect them. When it's time to go to work, jotting things down as they come in helps us remember them.

4. Organize our workspace

Remove any clutter or other potential distractions that may be interfering with our creative process. Sometimes try to swap workplaces to explore a different environment and get new perspectives.

5. Use lists to categorize our ideas.

Because we might have too many ideas rather than not enough, writing them down and categorizing them may help our best ones stand out.

6. Give it some thought.

Even if you assume that another cup of coffee would suffice, nothing beats a good night's sleep for a clear mind. Even a few hours of power sleep might help us reset our thoughts and continue our creative process.

7. Stop working and start having fun

Instead of straining to be creative for work, take a break and be creative for fun. Make something fun to remind ourselves why we want to create it in the first place, such as a painting, writing sample, graphic, or anything else.

8. Begin a tedious task

According to research, doing tedious labor boosts creativity more than simply doing nothing. Easy actions like housekeeping, listening to music, cooking, or any other simple activity can regularly stimulate new ideas.

9. Make errors and seek feedback.

Making mistakes and starting over is absolutely OK! If we're stuck for ideas, giving it our all and receiving feedback from others so we can improve in the future.

℘

Everyone has their own set of recommendations, as well as a few extra tricks that work well for them. Discovering our unique way of igniting our imagination is the key to breaking past our next creative barrier. When we're next gazing at a blank page, we can try one of these ideas, and maybe we can come up with our most innovative idea yet!

XII
EMBRACE THE CHANGE

"Every day the clock resets. Your wins don't matter. Your failures don't matter. Don't stress on what was, fight for what could be"

Change is an unavoidable element of life, and there is no getting around it. Change may be beneficial if it is well planned and implemented; but, even with careful planning, change is difficult to embrace, accept, and appreciate.

Kubler-Ross The Change Curve is the most dependable instrument for comprehending change and the stages related with it.

KUBLER-ROSS MODEL

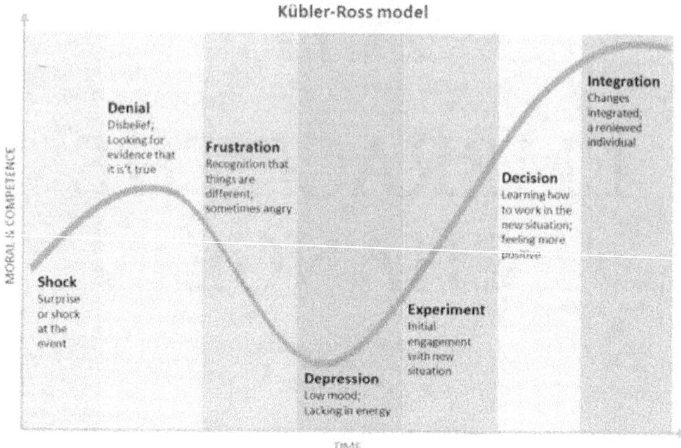

The Kubler-Ross Change Curve, often known as the 5 stages of grieving, is a model that depicts the many degrees or stages of emotions that a person experiences as he or she approaches death or is a survivor of an interpersonal death.

This paradigm includes five stages: denial, anger, bargaining, depression, and acceptance.

The five steps can be used in various ways and to varying degrees, depending on the individual. This paradigm applies not just to individuals facing personal death, but also to those facing less significant bodily issues or trauma. Injury, handicaps, employment troubles, relationship problems, and financial problems are examples of such scenarios or cases.

The Kubler-Ross Model also applies to business, work, and employment. Every firm must make adjustments to its management and policies. However, in addition to system improvements, there must be changes in individuals or workers.

Every business must assist workers who are undergoing transitions or adjustments. Individual transitions can be difficult, including a great deal of power loss and prestige concerns. The simpler it is for people to go on their path, the easier it is for the business to succeed. As a result, the company's success rate and total earnings are affected. It helps to fathom how one will react to change and how to provide support during the process of change.

$$\wp$$

THE 5 STAGES OF GRIEF

It is critical to remember that we do not progress through the phases in a linear or step-by-step manner. A person tends to progress through stages in random order and may occasionally return to a previous stage after a specific period of time. Each stage might continue for a varied amount of time, and it is conceivable for a person to become trapped in one stage and not progress.

Each of the five phases of grief is described briefly below:

DENIAL

The shock or denial stage is frequently the first in the Kubler-Ross Model and is usually brief. This is a stage in which you put on a temporary protective mechanism and take some time to comprehend any upsetting news or reality.

One may refuse to accept that what is happening is happening to him or her. It can reduce productivity and the capacity to thought and act. After the first shock wears off, one may feel denial and become fixated on the past. Some people might be in denial for an extended period of time and lose touch with reality.

෪

ANGER

When one finally realizes the enormity of the situation, he or she may feel enraged and search for someone to blame. Anger may appear or be conveyed in a variety of ways. While some people aim their rage toward themselves, others may direct it at others. While some people are upset with life in general, others blame the economy. During this stage, one is prone to become angry, frustrated, and short-tempered.

෪

BARGAINING

When the period of rage has passed, one may begin to consider methods to postpone the inevitable and attempt to locate the best thing remaining in the circumstance. Those who are not confronted with death but with another tragedy may attempt to negotiate the issue and reach a point of compromise. Bargaining may aid in the development of a long-term solution and provide some respite to people who are nearing what they desire to avoid entirely. During this stage, the quest for a different or less traumatic outcome may continue.

෪

DEPRESSION

Depression is characterized by feelings of sorrow, dread, regret, guilt, and other unpleasant emotions. He/she may have given up by now and come to a dead end where the route merely appears black. One may exhibit characteristics of apathy, reclusiveness, pushing others away, and a lack of enthusiasm for everything in life. This may appear to be the lowest moment of one's life, with no way out. Sadness, poor energy, feeling unmotivated, losing faith in God, and other symptoms of depression are widespread.

ॐ

ACCEPTANCE

When individuals recognize that resisting the change in their lives will not make the sadness go away, they submit to the circumstance and accept it fully. The resigned attitude may not be a cheerful place, but it allows the individual to stop opposing change and embrace it. While some individuals completely quit and enter a profound state of exhaustion, others may strive to make the most of the time they have left and seek other options. One has reached a state of calm and is ready to face whatever comes next.

FINDING MEANING

Grief is a normal reaction to the loss of someone or something significant to us. We may experience a range of feelings, such as melancholy or loneliness. Everyone grieves in their own way. But we can recover if we understand our feelings, take care of ourselves, and seek help.

There is no such thing as a "normal" period of time to mourn. Our mourning process is influenced by a variety of factors, including our personality, age, beliefs, and support network. The sort of loss is also a consideration. The grief fades with time. We will be able to experience happiness and joy in addition to pain. We'll be able to resume our normal lives.

When we are experiencing intense emotional pain, it might be tempting to try to numb our sensations with drugs, alcohol, food, or even a job. However, these are merely momentary distractions that will not help us heal faster or feel better in the long run. They can, in fact, lead to addiction, sadness, anxiety, or even emotional collapse.

Instead, the following activities can assist us in coming to grips with our loss and healing:

1. **Allow yourself time.** Accept your emotions and understand that mourning is a journey.

2. **Interact with others.** Spend time with family and friends. Avoid isolating yourself.

3. **Look for yourself.** To keep healthy and energized, exercise often, eat healthily, and get enough sleep.

4. **Return to your hobbies.** Return to the activities that make you happy.

5. **Participate in a support group.** Speak with those who are in the process of mourning. It might assist you in feeling more connected.

XIII

GUT FEELING

The sensation of "butterflies" in our stomach as we prepare to deliver a presentation, stress-induced stomach ulcers, emotional eating, and even our intuition manifesting as a "gut feeling" are all indicators that the brain and gut are linked and communicating.

The Second Brain: Our Enteric Nervous System

The network of nerve cells in the digestive system, which comprises 100 million neurons, is so extensive that it has earned the title "second brain." This network of neurons, known as the enteric nervous system, is commonly overlooked despite having more nerve cells than the spinal cord or peripheral nervous system.

Aside from the huge quantity of neurons, our second brain closely resembles our primary brain.

The extensive network of neuronal tissue in our stomach produces more than 30 separate neurotransmitters, which are signalling molecules that are normally linked to the brain. This includes an incredible 95% of serotonin production and storage, the neurotransmitter known as the "happy molecule" for its role in mood and wellbeing regulation.

Gut-Brain Crosstalk

So how do the brain and stomach communicate in real life?

The vagus nerve, the human body's longest cranial nerve, is made up of a thick cable of neurons that runs from the base of the brain to the gut. The vagus nerve serves as a bidirectional information highway, allowing the brain and gut to exchange information in millisecond bursts.

The vagus nerve is not the only link between the brain and the gut. The gut microbiota is made up of trillions of bacteria and other microorganisms that reside in our intestines. Because of the vastness of the gut microbiome, there are 100,000 times more microbes in our stomach than there are humans on the earth.

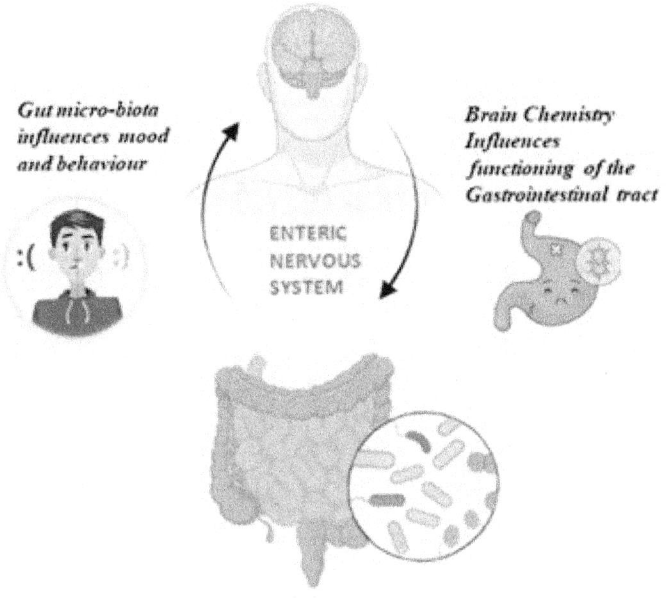

Many of these bacteria are present in the mucus layer that surrounds the intestines, where they come into contact with the bulk of the neuron and immune cells in our bodies. Furthermore, the vagus nerve is ready here for bacteria to take up on messages from the brain such as tension, concern, or even joy.

The organisms that make up our gut microbiota, on the other hand, are not passive. These cells generate modulating signals, which are then sent to the brain. Of reality, 90% of the neurons in the vagus nerve convey signals from the gastrointestinal system to the brain rather than vice versa.

This indicates that the signals produced in the stomach have a significant impact on the brain.

Brain Disease: The Influence of Gut Health on Brain Health

The interaction between the stomach and the brain helps to make sense of the accumulating evidence that the gut influences both brain health and disease. Numerous neurological illnesses have been associated to digestive issues or altered gut microbiomes, including schizophrenia, Parkinson's disease, Alzheimer's disease, and autism spectrum disorder.

Gut Feelings: The Role of the Second Brain in Mood Disorders

Inflammation, which is a distinguishing component of mental disorder, may explain the link between gastrointestinal and mental health. For example, a large number of people with inflammatory bowel illness also experienced worry and melancholy.

Both the gut bacteria and the vagus nerve are most likely involved in this. It has been shown that stimulating the vagus nerve decreases stress and inflammation, and some experts speculate that vagus nerve stimulation might be a novel way of drug-free antidepressant.

As a result, it is apparent that the stomach is more than just a food digesting apparatus.

ॐ

How does the gut microbiome affect your health?

We may be able to improve your gut health by making dietary and lifestyle changes. At least one of the following options should be tried:

1. Reducing our stress levels

Chronically high levels of stress are difficult on our entire body, including our stomach. Several methods for reducing stress have already been suggested.

2. Getting sufficient sleep

If we don't get enough or high quality sleep, our gut health may deteriorate dramatically, which can lead to other sleep issues.

Prioritize uninterrupted sleep for at least 7-8 hours every night.

3. Consume gently

By chewing our food thoroughly and taking our time at meals, we can lower our risk of obesity and diabetes and improve our eating habits.

This may help us reduce stomach discomfort and maintain intestinal health.

4. Keeping hydrated

Drinking enough of water may help us to increase the diversity of bacteria in the gut. Water drinkers had lower levels of a kind of bacterium that might cause gastrointestinal problems.

5. Taking a prebiotic or probiotic supplement.

Supplementing our diet with prebiotics or probiotics may improve our gut health. Probiotics are living, healthy bacteria, whereas prebiotics are "food" that promotes the growth of beneficial bacteria in the stomach.

6. Look for food intolerances

We may be allergic to specific foods. To see whether our symptoms improve, consider eliminating common trigger foods. Our digestive health can improve if we can identify and eliminate the meal or things that are triggering our discomfort.

7. Modifying our diet

Eating fewer processed, high-sugar, and high-fat meals may enhance your gut health.

A fiber-rich diet may also aid in the maintenance of a healthy gut flora. Consuming foods high in polyphenols, which are micronutrients, such as vegetables, fruits, coffee, tea, and wine, among others, may also benefit our digestive tract.

ॐ

4 Types of food for gut health

Diet and gut health appear to be inextricably linked. Because these foods may promote the growth of dangerous bacteria, avoiding processed meals, high fat foods, and foods high in refined sugars is likely essential for maintaining a healthy microbiome.

We may also eat foods that actively promote the growth of beneficial bacteria, so enhancing your overall health.

These foods consist of:

1. High fiber foods

2. Garlic

3. Fermented foods

4. Collagen-boosting foods

XIV

SELF-CARE

All the stress-relieving activities in the world won't assist us if we don't take care of ourselves. Meditation will be useless if we do not obtain enough sleep. In reality, when we try to meditate, we may fall asleep because we are not meeting our bodies need for sleep.

Self-care does not imply self-indulgence or selfishness. Self-care entails taking care of oneself so that we may be healthy, and well, do our work, help and care for others, and achieve what we need and want to do in a day.

Self-care encompasses all aspects of maintaining physical health, such as cleanliness, diet and seeking medical attention when necessary. It refers to all of the measures we can take to manage stresses in our life and care for our own health and well-being.

It has been characterized as a comprehensive, multidimensional process of deliberate participation in techniques that promote healthy functioning and boost well-being.

Essentially, the phrase refers to a deliberate action taken by us to enhance our own physical, mental, and emotional wellness.

Self-care may take many different forms. It might be as simple as getting enough sleep each night or walking outdoors for a few minutes to catch some fresh air.

Self-care is critical for developing resilience in the face of life's challenges that we cannot avoid. We will be better able to live our best lives once we have taken efforts to care for our minds and body.

Unfortunately, many of us regard self-care as a luxury rather than a necessity. As a result, we're left feeling overwhelmed, exhausted, and ill-equipped to deal with life's unavoidable obstacles.

It is critical to review how we care for ourselves in a variety of domains to ensure that we are caring for our mind, body, and soul.

❧

DIFFERENT TYPES OF SELF-CARE

Self-care is more than just finding ways to unwind. It is about caring for ourselves on all levels: cognitively, physically, emotionally, socially, and spiritually. To care for our health and well-being, we must strike a balance that allows us to treat each of these areas. Sometimes greater self-care in one area is required to restore balance or find respite from a stressor in our lives.

Physical Self-Care

We must take care of our body if we are to function properly, keeping in mind that our bodies and minds are inextricably linked. We'll think clearly and feel better if we take better care of our body.

Physical self-care consists of how we nourish our body, how much sleep we receive, how much bodily exercise we do, and how effectively we care for our physical requirements. Attending medical visits, taking prescribed medications, and monitoring our health are all examples of appropriate physical self-care.

Social Self-Care

Self-care requires socialization. However, it is frequently difficult to make time for friends, and it is tempting to forget our connections when life becomes hectic. Close relationships are essential for our well-being.

Investing time and attention in developing relationships with people is the most effective strategy to establish and sustain intimate relationships. There is no set number of hours we should spend with our friends or working on our relationships.

Everyone's social demands are slightly varied. The goal is to identify our social demands and to arrange adequate time to have an ideal social life.

Mental Self-Care

The way we think and the things we fill our head with have a big impact on our psychological well-being. Mental self-care involves activities that keep our minds sharp, such as puzzles or learning about a subject that interests us.

Reading books or viewing movies that motivate us may help to energize your mind. Doing tasks that assist us to stay mentally well is also part of mental self-care. Self-compassion and acceptance, for example, can assist us in maintaining a better inner dialogue.

Spiritual Self-Care

According to research, a religious or spiritual lifestyle is often a healthier lifestyle. Nurturing our spirit, on the other hand, does not have to entail religion.

It can include everything that aids in the development of a greater feeling of meaning, comprehension, or connection with the cosmos. Spiritual self-care is essential, whether we love meditating, attending religious services, or praying.

Emotional Self-Care

It is critical to have good coping skills while dealing with unpleasant emotions such as anger, worry, and grief.

Emotional self-care might involve activities that help us recognize and express our feelings on a regular and safe basis.

It is critical to include emotional self-care into our lives, whether we chat with a spouse or close friend about how we feel or set aside time for leisure activities that help us process our feelings.

ॐ

Why Is Self-Care Important?

A good self-care practice has been found to provide a variety of significant health advantages. Self-care is vital since it may assist promote health, prevent disease, and help us cope with illness. Self-care has also been connected to a variety of health and well-being advantages, including a longer life. Exercising, having a sense of purpose in life, and getting enough sleep have all been linked to a longer lifetime.

ॐ

Develop Your Self-Care Plan

A good self-care regimen should be adapted to our lifestyle and requirements. It must be something we produced for ourself. Creating our own self-care strategy can serve as a preventative tool to keep us from being overloaded, overstressed, and burned out. Determine which aspects of our lives require greater attention and self-care. And we must constantly evaluate our lives. As our circumstances change, so will our self-care requirements.

The following stages can assist you in developing our self-care plan:

• **Evaluating our needs:** Make a list of the many aspects of your life and the primary activities we undertake each day. Work, school, relationships, and family are a few examples.

• **Thinking about stressors:** Consider the parts of these areas that generate tension and how we may manage that stress.

• **Create self-care strategies:** Consider some activities that will help us feel better in each of these aspects of our life. Spending time with friends or establishing limits, for example, can help us form good social bonds.

• **Prepare for challenges:** If we notice that we are ignoring a certain element of our life, make a plan for change.

• **Start small:** We don't have to handle everything at once. Determine one simple move we can do to begin properly caring for ourselves.

• **Making time to focus on our needs:** Even if we don't think we have time for anything else, make self-care a priority. When we care for all elements of ourselves, we will discover that we can function more successfully and efficiently.

❧

The responsibilities of our everyday life might influence the sort of self-care we require the most. A self-care strategy for a busy college student who is always cognitively engaged and has a thriving social life may need to prioritize physical self-care. A retired person, on the other hand, may need to plan more social self-care in order to ensure that their social demands are addressed.

Self-care is not a one-size-fits-all approach. Our self-care strategy will need to be tailored to our specific requirements and what is going on in our life right now. We don't want to wait until we've hit rock bottom.

The idea is to take measures each day to ensure that we are obtaining the nutrients we require to deal with the stress and hardships of daily living.

Stress, Self-Care, and Productivity

We've known self-care by another name for a long time: recovery—just like how athletes recover from the pressures of training so they can stay injury-free and perform at their best on race day. And, just as certain forms of training are more exhausting than others, some types of recovery are more relaxing.

When we add just enough stress, but not too much, we increase fitness when we recover. If we do too much recovery without appropriate stress, we will lose fitness. This is based on the super-compensation concept.

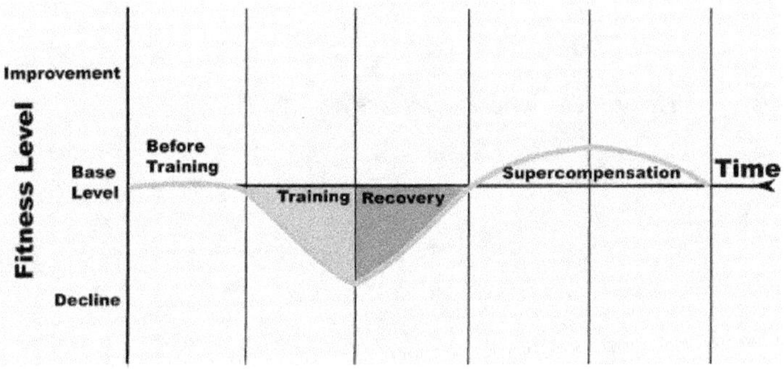

While super-compensation has many parallels with real-life outside of training, this model is insufficient for a coach's real-world pressures.

Productivity is another societal force that pulls at you that isn't part of being an athlete. It is that force that causes us to believe that **productive** = excellent use of time, and **unproductive** = waste of time.

THE SELF-CARE QUADRANT

We can try plotting our activities from the previous week on the graph in one of the four quadrants: energizing and productive, invigorating and unproductive, draining and unproductive, and draining and productive.

Where did we end up? Is there more activity on the bottom than on the top, or is there a decent balance?

What do you think about activities on the left vs. the right side?

We should observe these behaviors objectively and without bias. You could already be noticing things we'd like to alter.

"*Reflection is where progress begins.*"

By going deeper with a perspective can assist us in finding the proper balance.

Separated the quadrants into three categories: do more, do less, and our job.

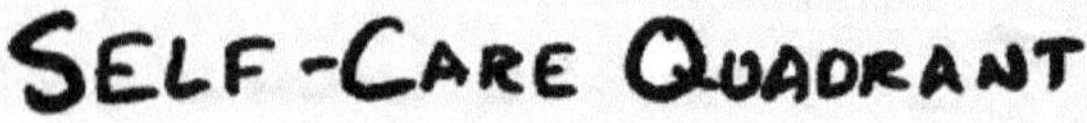

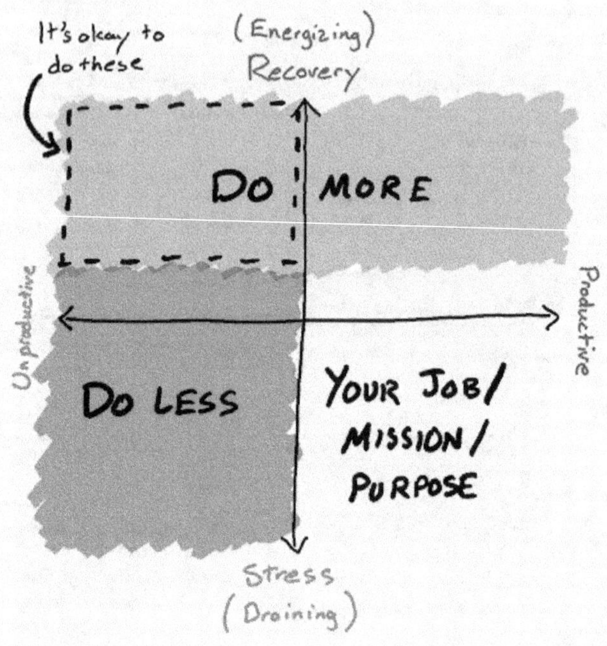

Our Job

Most actions linked to our employment and other responsibilities appear here. Many of these activities must be done, and most of them are physically, mentally, or emotionally taxing.

Do More

Energizing activities. Some can feel productive (gardening), and some not so productive (watching the sunset)

Do Less

Activities that are draining, unproductive, and marginally energizing, unproductive. It's no surprise that depleting, ineffective tasks should be avoided.

The self-care quadrant will help us to better understand how we spend our time. If we're having trouble keeping energized, we should consider the issues above and see if we can come up with any answers.

REFERENCES

The content for some of the chapters have been sourced from wonderful articles available on the internet, a few of them are cited below. Although i have tried to credit the respectful owners, Please feel free to contact me incase i forgot to mention your name.

❦

https://www.medicalnewstoday.com/articles/
323492#Whydo-we-get-scared?

❦

https://www.healthline.com/health/stress/effects-on-body

❦

https://www.bhagavadgitauniversity.com/blog/
bhagavadgita-summary-how-to-overcome-any-type-of-
fearkrishna-suggests-part-i/

❦

https://www.bustle.com/articles/165926-11-mental-tricksto-
help-you-conquer-your-fears-according-to-experts

❦

https://nursingeducationnetwork.net/2017/07/20/
thestress-curve-yerkes-and-dodson-law/

❦

https://www.albert.io/blog/arousal-theory-of-motivation-
appsychology-review/

❦

https://www.frontiersin.org/articles/10.3389/fmed.2020.00422/full

❧

https://whatfix.com/blog/learning-curve/

❧

https://www.mindtools.com/a9wjrjw/ebbinghaussforgetting-curve

❧

https://designgoodness.com.au/flowing-through-the-5-stages-of-the-creative-process/

❧

https://pearce.caah.clemson.edu/sparking-creativitycreative-block/

❧

https://atlasbiomed.com/blog/serotonin-and-other-happymolecules-made-by-gut-bacteria/#what-are-the-happyhormones

❧

https://www.businessinsider.in/science/this-is-why-ourphones-are-making-us-miserable-happiness-isnt-thesame-thing-as-pleasure-and-our-brain-knows-it/articleshow/63444829.cms

❧

https://www.healthline.com/health/gut-health#fa-qs
https://neuroscience.ubc.ca/our-second-brain-more-than-

agut-feeling/ https://www.simplypsychology.org/
psyche.html

ॐ

https://thedecisionlab.com/biases/dunning-kruger-effect

ॐ

https://www.simplypsychology.org/
maslow.html#:~:text=There%20are%20five%20levels
%20in,esteem%2C%20and%20self%2Dactualization.

ॐ

https://www.michaelswerdloff.com/anger-
secondaryemotion-what-protecting/

ॐ

https://rowhero.com/blog/self-care/the-self-care-quadrant-
a-check-up-for-rowing-coaches/

www.ingramcontent.com/pod-product-compliance
Lightning Source LLC
Chambersburg PA
CBHW071333140726
47996CB00005B/1960